D8

The Angler's Library

ESTUARY FISHING

Other books in
The Angler's Library

   Boat Fishing
   Canal Fishing
   Fly Tying, Rod and Tackle Making
   Sea Angling for Beginners
   Sea Angling: Modern Methods, Baits and Tackle
   Trout and How to Catch Them
   Coarse Fishing
   Salmon and Sea Trout
   The Angling Club Handbook

The Angler's Library

ESTUARY FISHING

F. W. HOLIDAY

BARRIE & JENKINS
LONDON

© 1974 F. W. Holiday

First published 1974 by
Barrie & Jenkins Ltd.
24 Highbury Crescent London N5 1RX

All rights reserved. No part of this publication may be reproduced in any form or by any means without the prior permission of Barrie & Jenkins Ltd.

ISBN 0 214 20041 8

Printed in Great Britain by
Richard Clay (The Chaucer Press), Ltd.,
Bungay, Suffolk

Contents

	Introduction	7
1	Shore fishing: general considerations; equipment and tactics	13
2	Boat fishing: the inshore dinghy and the workboat; seamanship and angling techniques.	25
3	Terminal rigs for shore and boat; leads, wirework etc.	40
4	Natural baits: feathers and spinners; pirks and plugs	55
5	Estuary bass	69
6	Estuary mullet	82
7	The flatfishes	92
8	Cod and whiting	105
9	Small fish and unusual fish	116
10	Estuary slob and sea-trout	126
	Index	139

Introduction

THERE are as many estuary types as there are rivers in Britain. According to the *Oxford Dictionary* an estuary is 'the tidal mouth of a large river'. Applying this definition the tidal mouths of smaller rivers and sea-lochs—which often have rivers at their landward extremity—are not estuaries. For the purpose of this study however we will define an estuary as being that area or region of any river where freshwater is directly influenced by the sea.

This question of saltwater influence is more extensive than might be supposed. Rivers which have a comparatively small fall from fresh to salt may be influenced for several miles inland. The advancing tide in effect dams these rivers and forces the freshwater back upstream. Thus you may witness the phenomenon of a tidal rise and fall of what is chemically pure freshwater. An example is the River Towy above Carmarthen.

There are mud estuaries and sand estuaries; estuaries beset by rocky cliffs and estuaries of Hollandic flatness. Vegetation may be profuse, as on the Teifi, with giant oaks leaning over the tide; or it may be sparse with the river meeting the sea surrounded by square miles of marram and sea-blight. Every estuary is different and each has its own secrets for the observant.

Estuary fishing has something in common with both sea fishing and freshwater fishing to which it adds special elements of its own. In a sense it is the great common hunting-ground where the selective fly-fisher can happily rub shoulders with both the coarse fisherman and the sea-angler alike. It is a place without great extremes, a sanctuary not greatly affected by the floods and droughts of the river nor by the tempests of the ocean. Generally frost-free and often remote, even in this mechanical society, estuaries are at once a refuge and a feeding-ground for a greater diversity of creatures than can be found in an equal area anywhere in Britain.

Listing the names of wild birds I have seen in estuaries is not one of my hobbies; it is enough to be aware that such birds exist and are about their activities. Even so, one would need to be very dull not to recognise a troop of greylag geese feeding on the saltings or to fail to spend a little time with binoculars watching a group of mixed waders to see if a rare specimen was present. And one would have to be even duller not to be astonished at the sight of a spoonbill knowing, as one must, that such a spectacle happens only once in a lifetime.

Fishing of course varies widely in river estuaries. Obviously it depends on what one is fishing for. Some estuaries are of interest only from the angle of sea fish; others are worth the attention of coarse fishermen; others again are highly productive from the aspect of game fishing, particularly for sea-trout. Most estuaries, however, generally offer mixed fishing for a variety of species although this is seldom exploited throughout its full spectrum and the true potential remains unknown. This is understandable enough since the dedicated pursuit of bass, flounders, sea-trout or whatever it is takes up the time and energy of even the keenest of anglers and leaves little time for experiment. It is true to say that almost any good-sized river estuary calls for a life-study to even partly understand it. And even then it will still produce surprises.

Since river estuaries are markedly affected by tides it behoves the angler to make a careful study of this solunar phenomenon. Tides determine not only the sport to be expected but such things as the comparative accessibility of an estuary and even the angler's personal safety. Perhaps it would be wise to stress the last first.

It is highly advisable to obtain a one-inch ordnance map of the estuary to be fished. Note the manner in which the sea moves inland at high tide, particularly on spring tides. If it threads a maze of gulleys and channels, as is often the case when the topography is soft mud, then extreme care is required when fishing. Such channels can be literally lethal if they fill with water and cut the angler off from the mainland. They are often impossible to wade or to swim due to the currents and their maze-like shape. Always play it safe when fishing gullied ground by first walking over your escape-route to make quite sure there is not some hidden but impassable obstacle. *Never* fish such places at night without a local guide.

Obviously a small craft such as an inflatable dinghy makes a big difference to accessibility and this aspect is discussed later. Accessibility usually varies according to the state of the tide and is best at low water. Some sandy estuaries are delightful to explore when the tide is out but are almost inaccessible at high water due to fringing beds of vegetation. Fortunately cattle often trample passages through this stuff and it is usually possible to find some sort of path up and down the shore. However I like to find at least two ways of getting out of these labyrinths well in advance of the tide because one may want to pack up at any of several points.

While on the subject of tides it is worth noting that tidal bores are not restricted to the Severn estuary; they occur, on a more modest scale, in quite a number of estuaries and tidal creeks. When a spring tide starts to flow on the River Taf in Carmarthenshire, for instance, the sound of the bore can be heard a mile away on a still day. It takes the form of a wave about two feet high—which sounds little enough until one realises that this is the distance between knee and waist. Bores should be treated with caution because some are bigger than others. Fortunately they are both visible and audible at some distance.

The range of fish found in river estuaries is wide indeed and almost nothing can be safely excluded, not even subtropicals such as the trigger-fish. I have known even such deep sea fish as blue shark to enter the seaward end of estuaries in pursuit of mackerel shoals. At the top of a summer spring tide it is not unknown for killer whales to come over the bar on the Teifi estuary and range around the tidal channel after seals.

Seals are quite common in some estuaries—too common in the opinion of many anglers. But this is not the fault of the seals nor of nature. Seals are naturally kept in check by killer whales but factory-ships have so decimated these whales that the whole ecosystem is now out of balance. Hence the Farne island butchery of seal pups which is really a clumsy attempt to put right trouble caused by the original interference. A killer slays a seal instantly by a nip of its great jaws and a shake of the head. This should be compared to the tortures inflicted by so-called seal hunters.

Even so seals are a real problem to estuary fishers. They sometimes range far up the tide and even enter the purely freshwater reaches. At such times the River Authorities are usually deluged with protests from anglers and netsmen alike. From the angler's point of view it is not so much the fish eaten by seals that is the problem as the fact that everything stops feeding when seals are around and the shoals scatter in panic. There is really no safe way of controlling seals except to encourage the killer whale to perform its function as nature intended. And that means supporting international legislation to stop indiscriminate killing of whales on the high seas.

Estuaries act as a nursery for the young of many sorts of sea fish. Tiny mullet, dabs, flounders, brill, turbot and many others can be seen swarming in the tidal pools of the saltings. This virtually endless supply of food is the magnet that attracts predators such as cod and whiting. At the same time the rich organic deposits attract such fish as flounders and mullet.

The superlative feeding in estuaries is the reason why they become the haunt of fish it is fair to call 'super-bass'. The reason for this will be entered into in the chapter dealing with these particular fish. This is an important aspect of estuary fishing and something we have come to appreciate only recently.

It may be a surprise to some fishermen to find that coarse fishing too has a place in estuary angling. Pike, roach and rudd seem to be invigorated by a tidal rise and fall provided the water remains fresh. On various occasions I have had excellent catches of roach on tidal parts of the Broads such as on the Yare and the Bure. The best roach I have ever had came from tidal water—a specimen of $2\frac{1}{2}$ lb. The lower Thames is also good, especially the pike fishing at Teddington Weir even though the tidal rise and fall is well over 20 feet. Estuary fishing for coarse fish, in my opinion, has not yet been studied half enough.

Pike seem to do well in tidal water and they are often described as a pest on the River Towy's lower reaches by salmon fishermen. Sometimes they are snared by bailiffs anxious to protect the gamefish. Sometimes the lower Towy changes its course and leaves a pool which is soon found to be stocked with pike.

One of the problems with estuary fishing is that it offers such a bewildering variety of sport that it becomes physically impossible to sample more than a small portion. Anglers tend to choose their quarry and settle down to years of pursuit of that particular species. Waters become famous for their flounders, cod, sea-trout or whatever it is that gets the most publicity. They could often be equally famous for quite different species.

It must be appreciated, too, that many estuaries—the majority—are comparatively remote and are not always easy to explore. Most of them are served by minor roads but these seldom lead to the best angling places. The fisherman will almost certainly have to leave his car and walk long distances over rough terrain in order to find out the fishing facts for himself. This is all to the good because it protects estuaries from over-fishing and exploitation by those who would turn every natural facility in Britain into a scheme for making money. Estuaries and their surrounding swampland are expensive to 'develop'—a term usually synonymous with 'ruin' —otherwise these watery wildernesses would have been concreted-over long ago. The fact that many survive almost unchanged from medieval times is a happy fact of benefit not only to the angler and naturalist but to all who delight in the countryside as nature created it.

As George Orwell might have said: 'All estuarial lands are owned but some are owned more than others.' The right of access to tidal water is often an exercise in judgement plus the ability to read maps. In England and Wales there are usually public fishing-rights in tidal waters although the angler may need permission to cross private land. If his quarry is sea trout he will also need a licence to catch this species from the appropriate River Authority. In practice, however, one finds that most estuaries can be fished merely by using common sense. This means having a word with local farmers and cottagers. By opening and shutting gates properly, avoiding standing crops and by being helpful to the country-side community the angler will soon make his face welcome instead of a subject for complaint. In such cases the niceties of legal ownership never arise and the fisherman is free to wander where he will.

In these days over-fishing is a problem almost everywhere. Estuaries however are one of the few exceptions to the rule.

There are various reasons for this. Anglers tend to take the easy option whereas many estuaries are not at all easy. The casual and lazy angler is soon eliminated when confronted by water, mud, poor roads and no shelter from the rain. Those who press on regardless will find, as the wild-fowler has already found, that the waiting wilderness offers compensations known only to those who are prepared to work for them. As for the others—it is better that they buy some bait at the shop and join the queue at the pier or local canal where everything is nicely organised.

True estuary fishing is not organised and I hope it never will be. This is the domain of the loner who is attracted more by the cry of the redshank than he is by the money prizes on offer in competitions or the crates of beer laid on for the organised outing. It is not everybody's cup of tea. Blank days can be numerous; and a blank day followed by a two mile tramp home through wet marsh can be pretty depressing. But at least the estuary fisher has no need to worry about charges going up, about take-over bids for water or being cramped for bank-space. And even when the bag is empty he can take away the satisfaction of being where sea, sky and river meet. After all, that is what it is mainly about.

CHAPTER ONE

Shore Fishing

Gear and Tackle

Shore fishing in estuaries can be conveniently divided into bottom fishing and spinning. Fly-fishing merits a separate chapter. Before considering tackle requirements, however, something should be said about the angler's clothing and personal gear because these can make or mar the sport.

Adequate footwear is essential if estuary forays are not to be miserable. This usually means a pair of clean woollen socks inside a pair of well-fitting thigh-waders. Sometimes it is possible to fish in ordinary gumboots especially when using a long oilskin reaching to the calf. The ideal outfit is probably thigh-waders, waterproof over-trousers and jacket topped by a sou'wester.

A strip of towelling to keep rain from getting down the neck and a pair of fingerless shooting mitts makes a lot of difference to comfort. In really rough weather I also carry a balaclava of proofed cotton. Obviously on a warm summer day much of the above may be neglected apart from the footwear although it is always a good idea to leave it at some convenient point—possibly in the car or at a friendly cottage —from where it can be collected if conditions change.

Regarding other useful clothing I have found nothing to beat ordinary denim jeans and an ex-army camouflage anorak. Both resist damp and are easily cleaned of muddy stains. Also they are cheap to replace. A spare pair of dry jeans and a pair of socks are well worth carrying if you travel by car. Incidentally don't be tempted to put wet socks on a warm engine to dry out—they are usually forgotten until the strange smell from the front is investigated on the way home.

Some anglers make a camping weekend out of an estuary trip. This can be fun and it makes possible the investigation of very remote areas. The use of a tent, van or estate car as a mobile base for estuary fishing can turn the sport into a much more interesting and ambitious a project than would otherwise be the case. It extends the angler's range and makes him self-contained. He can pick and choose the state of tide he wants to fish and rest-up when he feels like it. Most estuaries have some rough ground—often sand-hills—that can be used by campers.

The range of tackle required for shore fishing largely resolves itself into the question of which fish you seek and the technique to be employed. Freshwater rods and reels have their uses here especially if the quarry is flounders or mullet. A general purpose bait-rod which will be efficient against many of the species found in estuaries should have certain requirements which we will now examine.

A rod—any rod—is a combination of spring and lever. The weight, length and taper of a rod is determined not so much by the fish one hopes to hook but by the weight of the terminal tackle and the distance to be cast on average. Moderately long casts of 70 yards and over are sometimes necessary in estuary work. If leads of 4 ounces and upwards are being used then it is obvious that the sheer mechanical stress of casting demands a strong, lively rod of adequate length.

A strong rod, however, does not necessarily mean a heavy rod. Two-piece, fast-taper blanks are available made of fibreglass tubing making up to a total length of 10 feet. These fit into a 2-foot butt to give a 12-foot light rod of good casting performance using leads up to about 4 ounces. Blanks of this sort, to be fitted out by the angler, can be bought for about £6.

As regards rod-rings—it pays to fit the best. Nylon monofil line is tough stuff and when it starts to cut grooves in inferior rings not only the ring but the line itself has to be replaced. Rings with centres made from tungsten carbide will not groove and although they may be a little dearer than orthodox rings the extra cost is well worth while. Tungsten carbide is brittle stuff so a rod fitted with these rings should be given reasonable care. A pink deposit forms on tungsten carbide but it is harmless and readily washes off.

Few serious saltwater anglers use fixed-spool reels these days for bait-fishing. Multiplying reels are so vastly superior that one of these is the obvious choice. The one I use most often is a well-known American reel bought about ten years ago. If the reel is lightly oiled fairly often and kept quite free from sand and grit it gives little trouble. Since estuary fishing never entails pumping big fish up from great depths it is quite satisfactory to use a plastic rather than a metal drum on the reel. Being the lighter of the two a plastic drum is easier to control during casting.

Some anglers do seem to have difficulty casting with multiplying reels especially after dark. Most decent multipliers have some form of damping device fitted to mitigate against over-runs. It is certainly easier to have an over-run in the dark when the length and direction of the cast can't be seen than is the case in daylight. Obstructions behind, whether they be vegetation or a harbour-wall, also cause the angler to misjudge his timing and this could result in a 'birds-nest'. A policy I follow is to tighten up the damping device and sacrifice distance in the interests of safety. Supplementary brakes can be fitted to some reels which seem to be successful in preventing over-runs.

If you are going to whack a 4–6-ounce lead out over a tideway you will need a line of adequate strength. In fact it is usual to use line of two thicknesses—one of small diameter forming the main bulk of the line and a short length of larger diameter to take the shock of the casting action. The short length is usually called a 'collar'.

My own practice is to use about 200 yards of 15-lb. line on the reel terminating in about 14 feet of 28-lb. 'collar'. Some variation is possible here. You could use 18-lb. main line and a 30-lb. collar or 12-lb. main line and a 20-lb. collar. Which you use depends on the size of leads you use, the distances normally cast, the type of estuary-floor and other variables.

The collar is joined to the main line with a three-fold Blood Knot. To the business end of the collar is knotted a brass buckle-swivel or, better, a chromed brass quick-release swivel. A trace can be attached or detached from one of these in seconds even at night. Styles and designs of terminal rigs are dealt with in a later chapter.

Spinning can provide first-class sport in many estuaries but success calls for a good deal more know-how than does spinning in lakes and rivers in my view. Bear in mind that an estuary may extend eight or ten miles from its seaward cliffs to the limit of tidal influence and only a fraction of this water will be of use to the spin-fisherman. And when local anglers discover certain pools and stretches where interesting catches with the spinner can be made they seldom draw maps of them for the angling journals but tend to treat them as if they were gold mines.

For estuary spinning I use exactly the same tackle as I use for light salmon and sea-trout spinning. The rod is a two-piece fast taper glass blank with a long cork handle and movable reel-seating. This last is important because the balance of the rod, reel and spinning bait is critical if single-handed casting is to be accurate and comfortable.

A medium-sized fixed spool reel is used for this work. Some years ago I picked up a cheap Japanese reel of this type because it seemed well-designed, operated silently and efficiently and looked practical. It proved an excellent buy and is still in use. Bale-arms often give trouble with these reels. Even so there are more good fixed-spool reels on the market now than bad ones.

Many anglers hopelessly abuse their reels. Cleaning is an annual event and oiling almost unknown. Small wonder that bearings wear out and the wretched things become too stiff to turn. Reels should be top-dismantled after any trip on which they have picked up sand and be swilled under a fresh-water tap. Don't forget that wind-blown sand has a similar effect to dropping them in the stuff. When dry they should be lightly oiled and a little Vaseline smeared over the exposed surfaces. If this simple drill is followed your reels will last for years.

The thickness of monofil to use for spinning is a matter centred on the conditions. It can be as fine as 6-lb. up to about 12-lb. breaking strain. I normally use 8-lb. line but go up to 10-lb. if heavy lures are used or there are a lot of hazards such as floating seaweed. Let it be remembered that the thicker the line the less easily it will cast from a fixed spool reel. Also of course thicker line is a good deal more visible to fish—and this consideration is important in low clear water. The line must always be loaded so that it is level with the tip of the reel-drum or your casting will rapidly become inefficient.

A trace used for spinning should have three swivels built into it—one at the bottom, one in the middle and one at the top. The knot joining the reel-line to the top swivel should not have its surplus line trimmed but be tied so that about 1½ inches of surplus line hangs from the swivel. If a thumb-knot is tied on the end of this surplus and a bit of sheet-lead is bent over and clenched on the line it makes an effective anti-kink device.

It is futile to oil swivels, although it is sometimes recommended, because the lubricant is quickly washed away. Much better is to roll the swivels around on a tin lid covered with a stiff-bodied graphite grease. A water-resistant grease as used for pumps is best with graphite added.

FIG. 1. Trace for spinning.

Although there is a later section dealing with spinning baits it is worth mentioning that natural baits are not used half as much as they could usefully be. It must be admitted that this is often due to the laziness of anglers who can't be bothered to set up a natural bait but instead would sooner take an artificial bait out of a carton. Artificials have their uses it is true but natural baits are superior if only because they appeal to the predator's sense of smell as well as to its vision. Many anglers seem content to lure fish by vision only. Provided their quarry is keenly on the take they will do well enough. But if fish are not feeding too keenly then a bait which smells good (in addition to merely looking attractive) will succeed markedly over artificials which rely for success entirely on the visual sense.

This simple theory can be readily tested out with pike. Let two anglers of similar competence spend a day pike spinning. Let one rod be mounted with, say, fresh herring on a spinning-tackle and the other with a suitable artificial such as a spoon. Let the anglers exchange outfits every hour and book down every fish caught. At the end of the day it will be found that the natural bait almost invariably scores the highest total.

Exactly the same applies to sea fish. Anglers would be surprised and gratified if they knew the large number of fish that had shown an interest in their baits. Because, even in the best of conditions and even when using natural baits, only a proportion of fish do in fact take. There is really no doubt however that the use of natural bait increases this proportion; sometimes it increases it greatly. These are points to bear in mind when balancing the use of a convenience bait out of a packet against the chore of obtaining and mounting the real thing.

Where to fish

Bait-fishing from the shore in estuaries needs some planning and foresight otherwise it can be futile—and a very mucky futility at that. There are regions on many estuaries that just do not lend themselves to shore angling because of the mud. On the other hand I know of spots where the angler can fish while lounging on green grass surrounded by wild flowers. In deciding where to fish you need to have some idea of what you are fishing for. Mullet, bass and flats occur right up to the freshwater reaches. Cod and whiting will be nearer the sea. Mackerel and herring are somewhat intermediate and I have known both to occur—uncommonly it is true—several miles from the open coast.

I would never dream of trying to fish an estuary without taking a close look at the surrounds and the choices available. Topography counts for a lot. I know of one location where a 30-foot cliff fringes the river for a couple of hundred yards or so. This is a favourite haunt of anglers who sit in comfort among reeds where they hook plenty of flats, eels, mullet and even a few unofficial salmon. This sort of estuary fishing has gone on for generations.

An important characteristic to note is the depth of water at half-tide and flood tide. Some estuaries are wide and shallow; others are narrow and deep. All estuaries have a channel in which the freshwater flows when the tide is out. In shallow estuaries it is usually necessary to place the bait in or near this channel when the tide is in so that the main run of fish can be contacted. This channel tends to act as a highway up which fish travel as the tide rises so it is particularly important to know its exact location well in advance of the event.

Although the various species of estuary fish are dealt with later in this book there are some general observations which apply to all shore fishing in estuaries. Tidal currents in estuaries are often fierce and it is important to study their strength and direction and fish accordingly. Fish tend to enter estuaries on the fast central current and then fan out over the mud flats to feed. Having once arrived they don't seem to mind turning aside into quieter water. This is true of cod, whiting, mullet, bass and flounders. An interesting exception seems to be plaice which like rather fast water. All in all, the edge of the submerged channel is always a likely spot to drop a bait.

I'm sure this is a valid approach. For several seasons I made a sort of study of a tiny harbour out of which a stream flowed to form a small-scale estuary. Close observations from a flanking seawall were possible. It was observed that flounders were always the first to enter quickly followed by mullet and bass. Dabs, small plaice and dogfish waited for half-tide. Last of all, in winter, were the whiting. In fact it wasn't until dusk had settled before they ventured inshore. However in estuaries deep enough to hold 10 fathoms of water at half-tide you can catch these fish in daytime.

There is always an optimum period when fish take a bait best. It usually varies between half-tide and the first part of the ebb. It must be remembered that fish in estuaries are engaged in a mobile operation which includes a stringent time-factor. They have a strictly fixed period of time during which they must scout as much ground as possible searching for food before the ebb builds up to complete withdrawal of the sea. This means there is no time to waste and fish must go straight to their feeding areas.

How tight this schedule is was demonstrated many times when I fished the Taf near Llaugharne in Carmarthenshire. The moment the river-channel filled and the sea started to spill over across the mud flats the flounders were there in quantity. And hard on the heels of the flounders came the bass. Close behind usually came one or two porpoise to feed on the flats. What you saw was a whole food-chain in operation. It needed split-second timing because once the flounders had fanned out over the mud the porpoise could never have reached them.

Bass feed right up to the limit of the tide, often in water so shallow that their tails can be seen waving above the surface as they up-end to reach morsels on the bottom. Flounders and dabs are equally bold. This is often overlooked by beginners who feel that if they are not casting their baits a long distance they will catch nothing. In fact the reverse is often true; it is frequently the case that anglers over-cast rather than cast too short and the bait is dropping beyond the feeding fish. This is easily done and it certainly pays to begin the session with short casts and to lengthen them until the fish are found. This experimenting needs to be repeated fairly often because conditions are changing all the time as fish work their way back into deeper water at the start of the ebb.

Legering and paternostering are two of the most effective ways of fishing a bait in estuaries. Float-fishing, in my experience, is best used for the surface-feeding mullet. Float-fishing for flounders using a baited spoon has been described although I've never tried it. Drift-lining however is both interesting and effective. It is really a boat-fishing technique but can prove effective from the shore in certain locations.

I know quite a good spot for shore drift-lining. It is a 'neck' where a sandy estuary narrows between two rock ledges and then spreads into a wide haven. A light spinning rod is used. The terminal end of the tackle is merely a single hook baited either with lug or with a lask of mackerel. About four feet above the hook is positioned a few turns of lead wire. The length of the rod above the hook is a small plastic bubble-float half-filled with water.

The angler casts across the tide-stream and allows the bait to fish in a wide arc below him. Part of the time it will be dragging much too fast to catch fish but as it gets out of the main current it will stop dragging and start to hesitate in eddys and backwaters. These are the spots that fish tend to feed in because they act as food-traps. By varying the length of the initial cast, by paying out (and recovering) line and by wading, the angler can search a lot of water. It is an interesting way of fishing and can be very effective. Bass and flatfish are the usual quarry. However a preliminary survey of the area at low water is essential both to mark any possible snags and to examine any gullies and holes which may call for special attention as potential fish feeding-grounds.

An Imaginary Trip.

In order to give the beginner some idea of what shore-fishing from estuaries is like in practice we will set off on an imaginary trip. No particular quarry is in our mind on this occasion; all we are out for is some sun and wind coupled with interesting fishing.

Our tackle is a 12-foot rod of the sort described earlier. Our multiplier is loaded with 15-lb. line terminating in a 28-lb. collar. The tackle-box contains leads, swivels and quick-release fasteners of various sizes together with a spare spool or two of monofil.

We have never fished this estuary before so took the precaution last week of studying it at low water. The little river it serves is one of the lesser-known salmon rivers of the county. The middle portion is almost unfishable from land since it is mostly salt-marsh with banks of thick alluvial silt. Most rivers carry heavy sediment during spates and where it is deposited depends on the underlying rock strata which regulates the fall of the river. When a river has a rapid flow right into the sea the mud gets carried right into the ocean. Such estuaries are usually sandy or gravelly. The sea-bed offshore receives the sediment and often becomes a good ground for skate and ray. Incidentally, skate like clay ground, too.

Before planning this trip we bought a one-inch ordnance map covering this estuary and studied it carefully. The salt marsh is clearly marked as is the low-water river channel. Beyond the marsh and about a mile from the sea we notice that the banks become sandy and this is the spot we intend trying. A lane serving a few scattered cottages runs to within a hundred yards of the spot so carrying the tackle will be no problem. We will unfasten this gate and use it properly and then walk down by the side of the hedge. The farmer has wheat planted in this field by the look of it.

We planned our arrival to coincide with low water. This was partly to have a look at the estuary-bed and partly to try for a flounder in some of the deeper lagoons. The estuary here is a couple of hundred yards wide with the stream coiling slowly between the sand-banks. Groups of waders are busy and you could spend an amusing half hour with a bird book and a pair of binoculars looking for something to write to the newspapers about. However we have a more practical job—to deploy the flat-tined fork and rustle up a few lugworm. As you see there is no shortage of worm-casts. It is surprising how many fishermen crowd the foreshore digging for bait when a short walk up an estuary often produces bait in abundance.

Having crossed the sandbanks we notice a deep-looking pool on our left and decide to give it a whirl. When fishing off sand I always carry a plastic sack. You can kneel on it, sit on it and lay your reel on it without sand getting into the gears. Finally you can put your catch in it and prevent slime becoming spread around the car interior. Actually, I cut these sacks in two and use only the lower half after tying heavy cord to the corners so they can be slung over the back. In the spring farmers burn piles of these fertiliser sacks in the corners of fields so it's only a matter of uttering a word at the right time to be presented with a large supply. They are invaluable around boats, too.

Since the details of flounder fishing are discussed later we will skip that part and merely concentrate on the topography of this estuary. Notice the way the stream flows at the bottom of a deep centre gully between the sand-banks. This is caused by the water escaping and scouring away the finer sand. The current in this channel is always brisk— especially at the start of the flood and the end of the ebb. The fish in this fastish water are usually on the move and are not the best takers. Feeding fish seek the mouths of the numerous feeder-streams to find most of their nourishment.

Having caught a couple of flounders we decide to explore right out to the seaward end of the estuary. As you can see the shore is quite different out here. The sand has changed to grit and boulders. There are a few bladderwrack bundles lying around. Since this stuff moves in and out with the tides we'll have to avoid collecting too much with our lines. We take the opportunity here of marking out what seems to be an ideal venue. A small stream is cascading down the cliff and the resulting channel makes its way over the sand as a sort of miniature estuary. A formation of flat-topped shelving rocks juts out from the shore and makes both a good fishing platform and a safe retreat from the rising water. This looks to us to be a spot with a real fishing potential when the tide is in, especially for bass. We cast an imaginary lead with our mind then tramp over to where it falls and are pleased to see nothing in the way of snags, the ground being sand and grit with a few water-worn stones.

Our watch tells us that it is now dead low water. This being so we will walk just a little further and have a look at the bar—where the estuary gives way to the sea proper. The bar, as we now see, is simply a low sand-bank fronting the ocean. The bars of most estuaries are constantly shifting about and the sand is loose. This makes a hazard to be watched because it is easy to step into quick-sand or near-quick-sand and find your waders hard to extract.

The bar is good for many sorts of fish, especially bass. On some estuaries tope and the big flats such as turbot can be taken from such locations. Big plaice, too, like to haunt a sandy bar and specimens are caught every year all over Britain from this end of estuaries. Most of these fish are looking for sand-eels which are often prolific.

Extreme caution however is needed when fishing a bar, especially on spring tides. Examine the lie of the sand very carefully and make quite sure you can't be cut off. More than once I have been cut off on estuaries I thought I knew well because the levels had shifted since the last visit. I have heard anglers shrug such dangers aside on the grounds that, if the worst came to the worst, they could wade ashore. Of course sometimes you can. If you can see the bottom there is no problem. But if the water is too turbid to see the bottom it is very easy to flounder into a place where wading is impossible. The sea is quite indifferent to anglers who have made such a mistake and rescue helicopters fly hundreds of hours every season pulling people out of trouble they could have avoided.

Sand-eels around the bar nearly always attract some mackerel during the summer months. At the first lift of the tide it is not unusual for an entire shoal to cross the bar in order to attack the eels in the shallow water. The angler who wants to add a few to his mixed bag needs only to switch from bait to a small spinner and throw it over the shoal.

The tide is now at its lowest so we will linger here a little while casting into the surf for bass which often become very active at this period. We have already checked the exact route to be taken to safety once the flood starts. Since this is a small estuary we have decided to try and keep a little ahead of the tide and try dropping the bait into the channel the moment it starts to reverse its flow under pressure from the oncoming sea. These are good tactics for both bass and flounders. When mud stops further progress inland we intend finding one of the locations we marked earlier and settle down to a prolonged session which will include letting the rod fish for itself for a spell while we eat our packed lunch.

CHAPTER TWO

Boat Fishing

Choice of boat

The use of glass reinforced plastic and an upsurge of prosperity throughout the country made thousands of anglers who had never done so before consider owning and operating a boat for sea fishing. G.R.P. dinghies were being towed everywhere and launched with little idea of the rules of seamanship. Simultaneously, the coastguards were inundated with distress calls from small boats and the rescue services were in almost daily use. On the other hand quite small fishing boats that had been in regular use for twenty or thirty years were going out and returning safely with good catches of fish. So obviously there was room for a lot of people to acquire the know-how.

The beginner may assume that because estuaries are sheltered waters then they must be perfectly safe for 12- and 14-foot boats. Partly this is true. But it is also true that tidal flows in narrow waterways are extremely fierce especially on spring tides. The danger lies in this fact, not in the size of the waves. Until you become moderately skilled in the use of your boat, therefore, its use should be restricted to the slacker water of the neaps.

G.R.P. dinghies and clinker-built dinghies up to about 15-foot are easy to transport and launch. They are very mobile and draw little water. The special value of small boats of this sort in estuary fishing is the way they permit the angler to explore and fish tidal creeks and channels which are often totally inaccessible from land. Used in this way small dinghies are ideal for their purpose. They vastly extend the angler's range and make fishing possible in thousands of new and little-fished locations.

Boats from about 15 feet upwards usually have permanent moorings. They are therefore quite distinct from dinghies which are taken away with the owner after an outing. It is useful to categorise these bigger craft as 'work-boats' although, of course, any craft—even catamarans and yachts—can be used as platforms for fishing. Quite apart from its larger size and the probability that it has an inboard engine, the work-boat sits at an anchorage over a soft mud bottom when it is not out fishing or beached for painting. This means that you need a second boat—a tender—to reach your boat when it is afloat. Clearly therefore such boats are dearer to run and are a lot less handy than dinghies.

Whether you use a dinghy or a work-boat for estuary fishing depends on a host of factors of which cost is perhaps the least. Once you have a work-boat moored in a particular estuary, for instance, it is for all practical purposes restricted to that estuary. A mobile dinghy is not. The upkeep of a work-boat is certainly more difficult and some small job the dinghy owner could do behind his home in some odd moment may mean that the work-boat owner, to do a like job, will have to beach his boat and then refloat it. Moreover it is obviously wise to live at no great distance from your boat if she lies on a mooring so you can keep an eye on her. The expensive alternative is to employ someone part time to do this job on your behalf.

What are the advantages of a work-boat? Comfort is certainly a factor especially if you have done a lot of fishing cramped up in a small dinghy. It is also pleasant to have the room to prepare a bit of grub while on the water. A 20-foot boat drawing nearly 3 feet of water is obviously less handy in tidal creeks than is a dinghy. On the other hand such a boat can work the whole of the estuary no matter what the weather and its substantial engine will deal with anything the tides have to offer. Clearly however your fishing will now have to be more boldly planned. Because if your moorings dry out at low water you will need to either restrict yourself to relatively short trips while the tide is flooding or be prepared to lie over at the fishing grounds until the next tide.

After trying everything from small dinghies to heavy work-boats the compromise I find most useful is a 15 foot bass boat. It is a G.R.P. boat of Norwegian design. The towing trailer and engine were bought specially to suit the boat. A 5-gallon fuel tank—enough even for the longest day—is stowed in an aft locker from which point the fuel-line leads to a low-profile 6-horse-power engine. This boat is rated to carry five people which means, in practice, that three can fish in it and still leave room to spare. It has a speed of about 8 knots.

Other equipment

Every dinghy owner has the problem of launching and recovering his craft. Sloping ramps are provided at many resorts for this purpose although I personally prefer a flat beach. My own routine is to push the dinghy to the waterline on its trailer and then launch it over a pair of inflatable beach-rollers. The temptation to shove the trailer into the sea and float the dinghy off must be resisted unless you don't mind having trouble with your wheel-bearings. In any case I always spray boat and trailer off with freshwater on getting home and grease the bearings after every trip. The beach-rollers, by the way, are carried under the seats of the boat and act as additional buoyancy.

It seems hard to improve on this outfit in terms of a general fishing boat. Being completely mobile it can be launched at any point on the coast where there is beach access. There are oars for emergency use with flares in a water-tight locker as a last resort. The craft takes the seas well and will put the angler a mile offshore within ten minutes. If there is a more workmanlike answer to estuary fishing I have not so far come across it.

All boats, from the largest to the smallest, need good brakes. The brake of a boat is the anchor, and the old rule about having three times the length of cable needed to reach the bottom still applies. Modern anchors are more efficient than their old-time counterparts which means they weigh less and are more compact. I personally favour a four-fluke folding anchor weighing 10 lb. which is shackled to several feet of chain. The chain helps to provide the bite necessary to obtain a good hold. Nothing is more infuriating when fishing than to find that the boat is dragging her anchor and that you are creeping steadily off the mark. The length of the anchor cable depends on the depth of water you usually fish. I take along 30 fathoms.

Outboards are an efficient source of power both for dinghies and as auxiliary engines for work-boats. In that case they have to be mounted on a special bracket. If an outboard is treated with care it will operate without trouble for years. If it is not so treated it won't—the matter is as simple as that. For this reason I will never loan an outboard having discovered, after having to row four miles, that other people are often casual about these things. There are two important points about maintaining these engines and one is to mix the petrol and oil in the correct proportions. I use a good outboard oil and mix it in a proportion of 25/1 with low-octane fuel thus ensuring adequate lubrication under all conditions. The other point is to run the engine for a few minutes in a freshwater tank after every use in the sea. Care over these details is not too high a price to pay for faultless operation under what may be dangerous conditions.

Using the boat

The simplest deployment of a boat is to use it merely as a fishing platform. I know several anglers who do this regularly from work-boats sitting at moorings and they catch lots of fish without the bother of upping anchor and running the engine. The boat fishing techniques most commonly employed in estuaries are ground-fishing (which may be legering, paternostering or some variant), pirk and feather fishing, drift-lining, trolling and spinning. Which method you use depends partly on the species you hope to catch, partly on where in the estuary one is fishing and partly on the nature of the bottom.

It must be remembered that the estuary angler usually fishes what is regarded as shallow water. There are exceptions to this of course and some holes in Milford Haven, for instance, go down to 14 fathoms, but it is true in general. Therefore the fisherman will have no use for the heavy leads and wire lines commonly employed at offshore marks. Indeed he can often use tackle which would be thought too light by most sea fishermen. Glass fibre blanks of hollow section, specially designed for boat fishing, are not dear to buy and are easy to build. I use a 10-foot beach-caster with the butt sawn off which brings it down to 8 feet. For some sorts of fishing it is rather a powerful rod—when fishing for dabs at low tide, for instance. But all sea fishing is a compromise. Low tides are soon followed by flood tides and dabs are replaced by congers and bull huss so you have just got to split the difference.

Centre-pin reels are very pleasant to use for boat fishing and some anglers prefer them. They suffer from the disadvantage of having a slow recovery rate which is why, on the whole, I prefer a multiplier. Fixed spool reels designed for sea fishing can be used from boats but have no particular advantage over multipliers.

A hollow glass spinning rod of the sort described earlier, together with a small fixed spool reel to suit, is essential for the boat fisher when light bass-spinning is the order of the day. Such a rod can also be used for drift-lining and similar work. What it boils down to is the use of two outfits, one a good deal lighter than the other. There is a good deal of tolerance in what the angler naturally uses and he may quite possibly be able to adapt some existing tackle.

Finding a suitable mark for boat fishing in an estuary offers more available choices than a similar job undertaken in the open sea. The mark could, for instance, be 10 fathoms of water (measured at low water springs) for such fish as cod, whiting and skate all the way to the shallow waters of some tidal creek, with mud banks showing, where flounders, mullet and bass are the quarry. Shallow water work indeed may involve no mark as such but be more a question of roving. It may involve actually stalking the fish with the boat especially in high summer when they are much on the surface.

Deep marks are usually at the seaward end of the estuary but not invariably so. I've known some surprisingly deep pits to occur quite a long way inland. The only way to find such pits is by a mixture of experiment and chart-reading. Admiralty charts cover only those estuaries of interest to shipping. If an estuary is not covered by these charts a fair substitute exists in the $2\frac{1}{2}$ inches to the mile Ordnance Survey sheets. The value of a good chart can't be over-estimated since it helps the fisherman to pinpoint features such as wrecks which form the basis of a good mark.

Wreck fishing in estuaries is an aspect of the sport which has not properly come into its own. Many wrecks occurred around the coasts during the war of which little is known. The majority were small craft such as landing-barges and the like. A sizeable proportion were lost in estuaries while taking part in exercises or through hit-and-run raiders. It is true that many of these vessels are thick with silt and they are by no means easy to recognise for what they are even with a good echo-sounder. They are there nonetheless and attract their quota of fish tide after tide.

These mini-wrecks are not easy to locate because the ones dangerous to navigation have long since been demolished. The bigger ones are marked on Admiralty charts. As for the rest— the angler must either invest in a portable echo-sounder or resort to a series of parallel drifts trailing a bit of bent iron in the hope that it will foul the superstructure. Although primitive, this technique has enabled me to find wrecks in 20 fathoms of water and even bring up samples of weed growing on the hull.

Wreck marks are likely to harbour good cod, whiting, conger, pollack and ling. A food-chain is set up which starts with marine vegetation, passes to crustaceans and organisms of similar size which in turn attract various sizes of fish. These food-chains are self-renewing and never remain fished-out for very long. The best thing about a wreck mark is that it can't be trawled although it may attract professional long-liners.

Tackle, baits and lines

Fishing a natural bait weighted by a lead is the standard or traditional way of catching sea fish. Although more modern techniques such as the use of artificial lures and pirks try to supplant it they never succeed. This is not only because ground fishing is so effective but because it has a fascination of its own. There is something earthy about lowering a natural bait to fish that more sophisticated techniques never quite capture. This may be why so many small boys are attracted to baiting so early in life.

Boat fishing permits the angler to present his bait in a manner impossible to the shore-caster. He can use an extra long flowing trace—something the shore-caster cannot easily do. On the other hand, for quick-biting species like whiting, he can fish a paternoster tackle on a tight line and be in intimate contact with his quarry whereas the shore fisherman may need to strike along upwards of 50 yards of line.

Hooks are such an essential part of the fisherman's gear that it is worth considering them in detail. The range of sizes and shapes is now very wide indeed—so wide that even specialist hook firms can stock only a proportion of the total. It is important for the angler to form an early opinion about hooks and discover which sort exactly suits his needs.

My own preference for most sorts of sea fishing is an extra long, ringed, stainless steel hook made by Shakespeare, Redditch. Sizes 2 and 1/0 are the two most useful and these will deal successfully with many of the species to be encountered in estuaries. Larger sizes of the same hooks will deal with big cod and conger and smaller ones are useful for flats.

When non-stainless steel hooks become rusty the first place to be attacked is the point. Unless this is carefully honed fairly frequently it soon becomes blunt and useless. In my experience a fisherman careless enough to fish with rusty hooks is often someone who complains about lost fish but never does anything about it. Even when tying on a new stainless hook I always hone the point because there is really no other way of getting the critical degree of sharpness required.

I have heard anglers criticise long-shanked hooks as unnecessary. One hears the query: 'What is a long shank supposed to do?' Such anglers often use hooks with a sliced shank—the slices being a sort of barb intended to support the bait in position. This they do with tough baits such as squid but are much less effective with softish baits like razor-fish. It is a good idea to tie these baits to the shank with elastic thread. Trying to do this using a short-shanked hook merely results in loss of temper and a mess like a small golf ball. Moreover long-shanked hooks make it easier and quicker to recover the hook when it has been swallowed deeply.

For general ground fishing over a mark where mixed catches can be expected such as thornbacks, smallish cod, whiting, flats and so forth, I like to use a tackle which is a compromise between a ledger and a paternoster. It is simple in design and can be made up in minutes. The line is passed through the lead, and a bead followed by a swivel are knotted on to act as a stop. To the swivel is attached a 4-foot flowing trace with a hook at the end. This is the ledger part of the outfit. The paternoster part is simply a 6-inch snood and hook secured to the line about 3 feet above the lead. A smallish hook is preferred here—say a long-shanked size 2—because the paternoster part of the tackle is intended to interest shoal fishes such as codling and whiting which may be ranging some distance above the bottom.

When ground fishing it usually pays to adopt a broad approach even when you think you know the mark. A mark which may be swarming with whiting today may contain none of these fish tomorrow. Instead it may contain a scatter of thornbacks or even some common skate. Just as likely is the possibility that there may be nothing present but the ubiquitous dogfish.

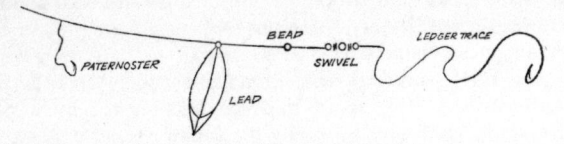

FIG. 2. Paternoster and ledger.

Ground-baiting is a valuable but little-used method of attracting and retaining fish over a mark. The main problem lies in streaming the bait into the water a little at a time at the right depth. Broken-up shore crabs, offal and crushed shellfish of various sorts all make useful ground-bait. The usual practice is to lower the bait in a perforated can or in a bag-net and to give it a shake from time to time. Many fishermen tie the bait-container to the anchor-rope but if the boat is riding to a long rope then the bait may well be attracting fish away from the boat. In my opinion it is much more satisfactory to put the bait down on a separate cord lowered from the bows of the boat.

As regards pirks and feathering—both methods are similar in technique and both employ artificial lures to simulate food-forms. However, whereas pirks are made of metal, feathered lures are constructed of hackles, hair, tinsel and sometimes plastic. Both types of lure are fished using a sink-and-draw action and both do best over fairly deep water. In an average estuary—if such a beast exists—this means fishing them over the centre channel on a flood tide. The construction of pirks and feathers is discussed later.

The method is ideal for use from a boat since the fisherman is presenting the lures to a quarry almost directly below him. He thus has far more positive control over the lures than does an angler casting from the shore or manipulating them from a pier-head. Pirks and feathers can be used whether the boat is at anchor or is on a drift. Indeed feathering (or pirking) on a drift is an excellent way of discovering new marks even though one may lose some tackle in the process.

Drift-lining is simply fishing a bait on a free-flowing, lightly leaded line. It has three important virtues the first of which is that the bait is constantly in roving motion and is likely to be spotted by fish over a wide area. Secondly, the motion of the bait—which is dependent on the tide-flow—is completely natural and therefore correspondingly attractive. Finally, the absence of any large amount of lead means that the angler is playing the fish rather than the fish struggling against a dead weight. Drift-lining therefore is one of the most sporting and interesting techniques that can be used in sea fishing.

The most convenient and one of the most effective baits for drift-lining is a lask of mackerel. Cut a thin slice from just above the tail about 2 inches broad. Then, using a sharp razor-blade, cut the slice into strips about $\frac{1}{2}$ inch wide. Pass the hook twice through the lask at its widest end so the lower part will undulate in the tide-flow. The main idea is to simulate the profile of a swimming sand-eel. To make a neat and realistic job you may need to trim away some of the mackerel flesh with the razor-blade in order to get a really lively effect.

FIG. 3. Driftline rig.

Even better than mackerel-lask is the 'real thing'—a live sand-eel afixed to the hook by passing the point through its mouth and out at the gill. Other useful baits for drift-lining are smelts, lasks of herring or the tail of a small freshwater eel. These last are quite a good bait and can often be found under stones on the beach.

Lead is needed to take the drifted bait down to fishing depth. Since the amount of lead will vary according to the strength of the tide-flow it is essential to use a series of small leads which can be added or removed quickly according to conditions. This selective approach makes drift-lining a most attractive form of fishing because the range of quarry is so wide. Bass are the prime target with many anglers and there is no more sporting method of catching them than on the drift. However they are only one possible species out of many. There are three zones in the sea—upper, middle and lower—and each tends to contain fish appropriate to the zone. By adding or removing lead from the drift-line the angler can fish from zone to zone and thus seek out some particular quarry.

Trolling

Trolling from a boat is a method of showing a bait to the maximum number of fish. Artificial lures are commonly used for this work such as plastic or rubber sand-eels, scaled spoons or metal sand-eel simulations like the 'German sprat'. Some anglers prefer to use a large lask of mackerel. The main point about trolling is that you cover a large area of water and it is a good method to use in a little-known estuary on a speculative basis.

Much of the success attendant on trolling depends on using a good trolling speed. Most boats tend to troll too fast. The correct speed is a nice balance between the speed of the tide, the amount of lead on the trace (or weight of lure) and the depth of water. In deepish water, as a general rule, I like to get the bait down to about 10–15 feet deep and keep it there. A slower boat-speed permits a reduction in the amount of lead on the trace and vice versa. And of course in shallow water the quantity of lead may have to be greatly reduced.

Some anglers prefer to use the engine for trolling whereas others would rather row. Rowing admittedly allows you to troll at a very slow speed indeed and also in silence. Myself, I would sooner use the engine having found that the slightly higher speed makes no difference to the number of takes. However, if you intend doing a lot of slow trolling it is most important to have a well-tuned engine and carefully-mixed fuel if one is to avoid trouble with the sparking-plugs. The slow-running jet must be clean and properly adjusted. Even so, I find it advisable with the engine I use to give it a burst of power every ten minutes or so. This helps to clear the plugs and prevents trouble arising.

Plenty of line should be allowed between the boat and the lure. Fifty or sixty yards or more is usual. Some anglers pay out over a hundred yards but I don't think this advisable. Nylon monofil is very elastic stuff and the amount of stretch in a hundred yards is considerable. This is not so important when fishing with static natural baits because fish will tug hard at baits again and again. When using artificial lures, however, they usually attack once and once only. Unless you can fix the hook first time that is probably the only chance you are going to get. It is for this reason that some anglers prefer non-stretch terylene lines for trolling.

It seems hardly necessary to add that trolling rods must be made secure when they are fishing. However, after a long blank spell it is awfully easy to become casual about this. It is an expensive reminder that this is not a safe practice when one sees a rod whipped clean overboard by a taking fish. Quick-release clips of various sorts can be fitted but personally I prefer to hold the rod at all times.

Spinning

Casting and spinning from a boat is a very effective way of taking such fish as bass and mackerel which collect in shoals. Stalking these fish while afloat is a fascinating way of fishing and calls for a good deal of skill in both casting and boatmanship. It is easy for an inept boatman to scatter and disperse such a shoal. Excessive use of the engine of course soon has an unsettling effect on such surface-feeders and a final approach using oars is best.

Spinning is particularly effective when you can get the boat on a drift using the incoming tide when a shoal is also moving in with the tide. It is sometimes possible to position the boat with the oars or a bit of sail so that one can cast to completely undisturbed fish. In these conditions it is a mistake to cast the lure across the shoal so that it travels through the middle. The fish become uneasy—possibly because many encounter the swivels and anti-kink and don't like them. Always try to cast to the fringe of the shoal and draw the lure away from it.

Spinning from an anchored boat is also a useful ploy. I

find it especially effective when the craft is moored within casting-range of some likely lurking place for fish. This could be rocks, a pier staging, a waterlogged hulk or whatever. If the location is a tidal backwater and out of the main run of the current it often pays to anchor the boat using a killick. Most killicks or rough-ground anchors are made from flat stones. Some fishermen prefer to make a cement block with a ring attached. Killicks are invaluable to the dinghy angler for drifting a few yards and then stopping. By lifting the killick quietly clear of the ground the boat will then glide to a new location thus enabling the angler, as it were, to sneak up on the fish.

FIG. 4. Two types of killick.

The light spinning tackle already discussed is used for this work. The choice of suitable lures is a wide one. However, it pays to avoid the rather fragile lures used in freshwater spinning because salt will quickly ruin them no matter what precautions are taken. Choose a spoon having substantial weight for its size and be sure the treble hook and the rings are, if possible, of stainless steel. The colour is not critical but dark blue and silver is particularly effective for bass. For deeper swimming fish I prefer yellow and silver because yellow shows up better at depth.

The traditional lure for spinning in the sea is the rubber or plastic sand-eel. The orthodox design is a single-piece eel sometimes with a mackerel-spinner mounted on the nose. Modern eels, such as the Red Gill, are far superior to the old-time baits both in appearance and in performance. An angler who is very successful at spinning for bass makes his sand-eels in two sections out of soft plastic with a single 2/0 hook mounted on the underside. A homemade pattern I have found very effective is described later.

These comparatively light baits need to be slightly weighted for casting. A small anti-kink lead, mounted in front of the nose, is usually sufficient. Even so, it will probably be necessary to pause for a few seconds after casting before winding the eel back to the boat. If one is after pollack quite a long pause may be needed because this species usually lies deep. Wind slowly and steadily with the occasional pause remembering that fish often stalk a bait before seizing it.

An important point about lures, especially homemade lures, is that they tend to vary slightly and this greatly affects their fish-catching properties. The only way to distinguish a good lure from one not so good is to fish it and find out. It will be found that some are complete duds and have to be scrapped. Some, I am convinced, actually succeed in scaring the fish rather than attracting them. Occasionally you will make an eel or a spoon that is so deadly that it catches fish on almost every occasion. I am convinced that vibration has something to do with these results because many predators hunt their prey by detecting the vibration rhythm made by their quarry. An artificial sending out a wrong rhythm may be as off-putting to the fish as it would be to us if we sat down to ham and eggs only to find that the dish smelled of sherry trifle.

Commercialism versus conservation

Any angler owning a boat and fishing from it successfully will encounter the commercial aspect of sea fishing. Bass and other prime fish have a ready sale to cold storage companies. As prices move upwards and it remains a fact that almost every species is marketable there is a temptation to join the growing number of weekend fishermen whose main idea is to forget the sport and work on the business. Over-fishing is not a problem that is getting any better.

Some beaches are regularly swept by seine-nets and this certainly does nothing to improve the bass fishing which often deteriorates to the disappointment of tourists who have spent good money to enjoy the angling. *Pro rata* a bass available for catching by visitors produces far greater economic gain to a community than does a bass captured by a netsman. Exactly the same argument applies to salmon. Yet there is no government policy to limit the killing of either species or to make the best economic use of what we have available. The system still operates as it did in medieval times.

Over-fishing is not of course confined to bass. The owner of a small boat was recently fined £25 for bringing ashore a quantity of soles smaller than 25 cms. long At a resort well known to me it is commonplace to see undersized plaice and other flatfish being landed, usually at night. As for amateur trawler-men—there is really no check on those who find it profitable to drag a small trawl around close inshore.

The fact is that the laws relating to the seas around our shores are hopelessly out-of-date. Those of us who were writing about the dangers of pollution in the angling press twenty years ago have lived to see the nation slowly become aware of the situation. I have no doubt that this will be so over conservation. By insisting on restraint by fishermen at the Icelandic fishing-grounds the Icelanders have done the world a service. The greedy inroads being made at the ground by ships of various nations, including Britain, would have rendered the grounds barren within a measurable time.

All shallow sea (under 5 fathoms at the bottom of spring tides) should be designated as conservation areas in which trawling of all sorts and seine-netting were not allowed. Long-lining and angling would be permitted but with closer checks on the size and numbers of fish retained. There might be exceptions for certain prolific fishes such as herring and mackerel. These banned areas could easily be rendered unfishable to trawlers by a system of underwater obstacles. Artificial reefs made of discarded car-bodies and similar scrap have already proved their worth in some parts of the world and the idea should be taken up around Britain without delay.

A serious and vigorous conservation of fish-stock is of advantage to everyone—to the nation, the professional fisherman and the angler. If many of the species now familiar are seriously reduced in numbers—and this seems inevitable—then everyone is the loser. On the whole anglers are aware of the situation just as they were aware of pollution twenty years ago; this awareness needs extending widely and quickly. The hundreds of sandy bays around our coasts are particularly vulnerable to these commercial depredations, especially to beam-trawlers which leave behind them a sterile legacy of plough-up sea-beds which take years to recover. To continue like this is madness when mankind faces the greatest protein problem in its history.

The only alternative to conservation must be synthetic food. Fat plaice and plump soles will come to be delicacies our grandfathers enjoyed and they will take their place beside quail, bustard and similar historical dainties. Soya meat (fish flavoured) will be our last lingering look at the treasures of the sea we failed to husband in time.

CHAPTER THREE

Terminal Rigs

Terminal gear

Terminal gear for shore fishing in estuaries must be suitable for a range of different conditions, from surf-casting on an open beach to fishing in calm brackish water several miles inland. Clearly quite a different sort of tackle presentation is going to be needed in these two extremes as well as in various intermediate situations. In fact I know a location where the angler may encounter such variations within half a mile. He may, for instance, be fishing in the surf of the open beach at one stage of the tide only to be fishing into slack water from a mud-bank at another stage. Such contrasts are by no means unusual when estuary fishing.

Many anglers fail to appreciate that casting into surf is rather like fishing in a boiling cauldron. To leger with a long flowing trace when the waves are pounding on the shore is just about useless because the trace will spend its time lashing about like a mad snake. Nothing is served by making it as hard as possible for fish to find and devour the bait yet I have seen anglers doing just that.

Practically every experienced fisherman has his own ideas about terminal rigs and experiments constantly. Some use a single hook for surf-fishing; others use multiple hooks. Personally, I prefer a pair of hooks because this acts as an insurance against fishing without bait should one of them shed its bait during casting. At some locations there is the chance, too, that the bait may become covered with sand or be concealed by weed. If this happens when using one hook you are quite literally wasting your time.

For general surf fishing I use one of two variants of the same rig. Type A is made up as follows: to a swivel is attached 2 feet of monofil line which is threaded through the loop of the casting lead and stopped with a bead and a second swivel. The lead thus has an uninterrupted run between the two swivels. The upper hook is tied to a 4-inch snood attached to the lower eye of the topmost swivel. The lower hook is tied to a 9-inch snood attached to the lower eye of the bottom swivel.

The threshing effect produced by heavy surf which often tangles even short snoods around the main line is guarded against by stiffening the snood. One way of doing this is to

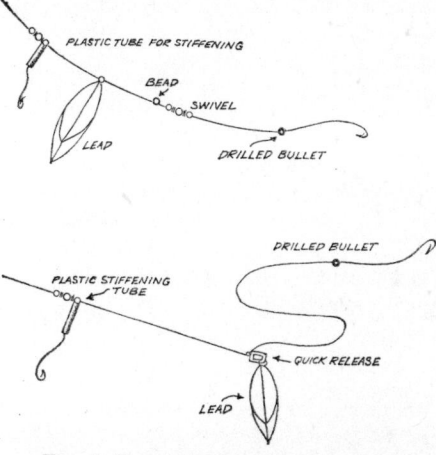

FIG. 5. Terminal rigs for surf-casting.

slide a length of fine nylon tubing up the snood before tying on the hook. Just as effective is to whip a nylon 'bristle' taken from a stiff broom to the snood and secure it with fly-tying silk. Of course a bit of really heavy monofil will serve the same purpose but great care needs to be taken that the knot is secure. Ball-point pen tubing can be used although it is rather coarse for the job. Fine tubing is available from some tackle-shops who supply it for making tube-flies. The lower snood of this rig lies on the sea-bed. Instead of using tubing to stiffen it one can, instead, use a ¼-ounce drilled bullet and this has a similar effect—the tackle is made inert and kept from lashing about and producing tangles.

The Type B rig is made up as follows: to a swivel is attached 2 feet of monofil line as before. Instead of threading it through a lead and stopping it with a swivel however the 2 feet of line has a quick release snap swivel tied to its lower end. A lead is snapped into the spring of the quick release. The upper snood is constructed as before and attached to the lower eye of the upper swivel. The lower snood however is tied to the upper eye of the snap swivel.

The motive for this is simple enough. When conditions are relatively stable it is often convenient to use Rig A with a lead built into it. But on big tides when a variety of leads is likely to be used during one session the second rig is a lot handier. For instance you may start fishing at low water using no more than a 2-ounce bomb, progress to something bigger and then have to end up using leads of between 4-6 ounces. You may need to use spiked leads. The snap release makes these changes easy. It follows that the Type A rig is most likely to be useful on quiet neap tides and Type B on turbulent spring tides although there is no rule about this and a lot depends on the weather, the amount of ocean surge and other factors.

It also seems to me good policy to secure the bait to the hook. This is especially the case when relatively soft baits such as razor-fish are in use. After some experiment with mechanical clenching devices, tiny nylon bags and other gadgets it seemed to me that the following essentials had to be fulfilled: (i) the bait must be fully exposed to the fish, (ii) the securing device must be both positive and simple and (iii) it must be easy to operate under adverse fishing conditions.

These ends seemed to be achieved by tying a 4-inch length of elastic thread to the eye of the sea hook. To the end of the thread was tied a Size 12 freshwater hook. After baiting the main hook with razor or other softish bait the elastic thread was wound tightly around the bait and finally spiralled up the shank so that the freshwater hook could be slipped under tension through the eye of the main hook. Although simple and inexpensive the device worked reasonably well in practice and certainly saved bait. Even so, an efficient bait-retaining device that is both light and neat will make a fortune for anyone who puts it on the market, so one hopes that experiments will continue.

For fishing in relatively slack water from the shore I usually use the simplest form of leger. A 2-foot length of monofil is secured to a swivel and a suitable hook is tied to the other end. The main line is threaded through the eye of the lead and then tied to the swivel. This simple rig can be made up at the waterside and it is useful when fishing with crab. In that case I often use a treble hook and a 'crab board' as described below.

A good case can be made out for having the lead attached by a much more free-sliding arrangement than that pro-

FIG. 6. Bait retaining device.

vided merely by passing the line through the loop of the lead. This calls for a certain amount of what sea-anglers term 'wire-work'. A modified Clements Boom is probably the most positive device and it permits bites to register when the pull is exerted at a variety of angles without disturbing the lead. The boom is slid on to the line above the single swivel and the lead is attached by the clip provided.

Home-made wire-work and leads

Under the term 'wire-work' must be included various quick-release devices, screw-links, paternoster booms, spreader arms and many more. Such devices are easy and cheap to make even by those with only a small amount of manual skill. Moreover by making them yourself you can easily incorporate small refinements and variations which experience suggests are helpful to one's method of fishing.

Brass wire or stainless steel wire can be used. Brass wire of suitable gauge can be obtained from any welder. It offers the advantage of being readily soldered and thus enables the eyes and joints to be finished off very neatly. Wire-work is becoming increasingly dear to buy and some of it is far from ideal. It constantly surprises me that more anglers don't produce their own wire-work especially since the job is so simple. The only tools needed are a small bench-vice, pliers and a soldering kit together with a steel tube of small diameter to slip over the end of the wire and use as a lever.

Home-made wire-work can be as robust or fine as the angler wishes. Chromed brass swivels are built into the constructions as desired. If the angler wants to turn out a series of some particular item it is quite easy to make a metal or plywood template around which the wire can be bent to ensure uniformity.

The basic principle behind all wire-work in modern sea fishing is neatness and economy of material. It is better to use too little wire or none at all than too much. The day of the primitive 'sea paternoster' with its ungainly links of large diameter wire connected by huge swivels is over and most anglers regard such contraptions as Edwardian museum pieces. Where there is a lighter and neater alternative to wire then it should certainly be used.

Paternosters today are usually very simple tackles made up by forming a spaced series of loops in the trace—usually three—by means of Blood Loop Bights. A short snood of slightly weaker line carrying a hook is tied to each loop. The lead of course is located at the foot of the tackle. Thousands of fish are caught each year on such rigs. They have the advantage of being made up easily at the waterside from stock material and for such shoal species as, for example, whiting there is little to beat them. The loops of course can be quite widely spaced on a long trace if the angler wishes to fish simultaneously at several different levels.

The only possible advantage the old-time wire paternoster had over the modern rig is that, since it incorporated spreadarms, it avoided 'round the trace' tangles. Clumsiness however is a high price to pay for this advantage. Personally, if I want to hang the snood well away from the main line I use a 4–5 inch length of stiff plastic tubing. This is drilled with a 1/32-inch drill and the trace is passed through it. A small swivel is tied into the trace at the appropriate place and the plastic boom rests on it. In the interests of security I always pass the snood through the middle of the boom and tie it to the main line.

Many variations of this sort are possible and local anglers often produce well-designed rigs which are marvels of ingenuity and slanted at conditions prevailing in local waters. Any experienced sea angler who offers to show you the tackle he has made should have his offer gratefully accepted. Some chaps are secretive and decline to discuss their rigs or allow

BLOOD LOOP BIGHT FOR FORMING SLIP-PROOF LOOP

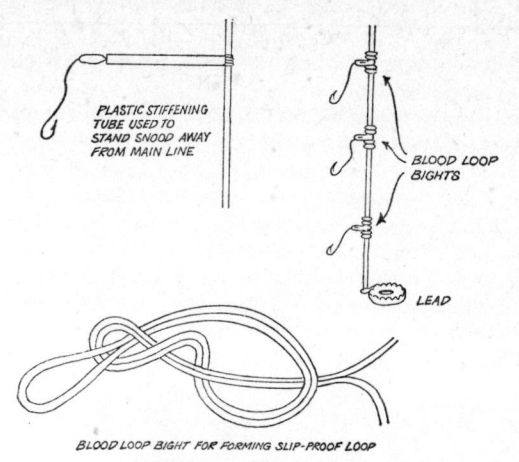

FIG. 7. Paternoster rigs.

them to be photographed. Since it may have taken them years to devise the stuff this attitude is not unreasonable.

Paternosters are useful whether fishing from boat or shore. This is not so with the drift-line which is entirely a boat technique although it can be used from pier-heads. Essentially drift-lining consists of streaming the bait down a tidal current. It is really nothing more than a baited hook deployed on a freely moving line and many boat anglers favour it as the ideal way of offering a bait to fish in the most natural manner possible. Live sand-eels, prawns, thin lasks of mackerel and other titbits can be presented in this way as already described. A small amount of lead is used to keep the bait at fishing depth, the lead being clenched to the upper eye of a swivel to permit free rotation of the bait. A cutaway anti-kink lead is most useful for this job. These are easily made out of lead sheet.

This brings us back to the home workshop aspect again. Most serious sea anglers do in fact make their own leads. They use either one of the machined aluminium moulds which are readily available—by far the easiest method—or make their own moulds. Casting leads for sea fishing is easy enough and it reduces the cost of replacements considerably. I use an old soup-ladle for melting the scrap lead; also gloves to avoid burns. Metal moulds need to be heated before lead is poured into them and it is a good idea to smoke the inner surfaces of the mould with a candle-flame to prevent the casting sticking.

The estuary angler will need three or four different types and sizes of leads. For general surf-casting on the open shore he will require a few 4-ounce Torpedo leads. If the surf is heavy, however, these may tend to roll inshore and an anchor lead with wire legs which dig into the sand will have to be substituted. The best pattern of anchor lead are the 'Breakaway' type, the legs of which collapse on recovery and thus reduce drag (see Figure 11). For boat work I use either a plain Torpedo or a 'Grip' lead in the 3–4 ounce range. In a tin box you will need to carry a supply of fold-over, anti-kink

FIG. 8. Grip lead.

leads of various sizes for use in drift-lining. Finally, in another box, you will need a supply of drilled bullets and swivelled bombs in sizes ranging from ½–2 ounces. Moulds are available to cast these small leads in batches of half a dozen.

Most leads of the Torpedo and Grip type incorporate a loop of brass wire with which they are secured to the terminal rig. Some anglers simply tie their lines to this loop whereas others prefer an attachment incorporating a swivel. If you make your own leads it is easy to slip a swivel on to the loop before pouring the lead into the mould. Alternatively one can use a quick-release with a swivel built into it. It is certainly a big advantage with many sorts of leger rig for the line to slide freely through the lead when the fish seizes the bait. Not only is the bite registered more easily but the fish, feeling no resistance, is more inclined to take the bait.

When ground fishing for flatfish I like a Grip lead with a $\frac{1}{16}$-inch hole drilled to pass through both sides of the lead in the horizontal plane. The line is threaded through the hole and a swivel is tied on. Below this is a long flowing trace carrying a couple of hooks. Such a rig is useful for flounders and plaice.

Hooks

The matter of hooks is critical when making up terminal rigs. It cannot be too often repeated that a sound, really sharp hook is the most essential part of the angler's outfit. Fish can be landed on weak lines and inferior rods and reels but if the hook is faulty then the outing is automatically a failure. The problem is a real one for the estuary fisher since not only must he contend with the effects of saltwater but he must also guard against his hooks blunting on stones and it is extremely easy to suffer this hazard.

Amazingly, many anglers are quite content to take a new hook from its packet and tie it on the tackle without giving a thought as to its sharpness. The fact is that new hooks are *never* sharp because production methods do not permit hooks to be individually honed which is the only satisfactory way of achieving this result. Those with coarse barbs may even have to be filed although it is better not to buy such hooks in the first place. Some anglers hone their hooks to form a square or a triangular section at the point but I think this is a mistake. For most fish it doesn't really matter. But if you are fortunate enough to hook a specimen on light tackle and the playing of it is a lengthy process then the angular honed edges may tend to cut laterally so that eventually the whole thing merely drops out in spite of the barb. If one aims to produce a needle-sharp conical point with the hone then all is usually well.

Hooks are usually made of rust-protected steel or from stainless steel. The rust protection—generally a deposition process such as 'bronzing' or galvanising—has a short life in the sea and it is necessary to replace such hooks fairly often. Stainless steel hooks are handy in that one is saved the trouble of having to replace hooks in existing tackles. These hooks have a good point and hone to an even better one. They are available with shanks of various lengths and are made from a good thickness of wire without being over-clumsy. So-called 'nickel-plated' hooks, in my experience, deteriorate rapidly in saltwater and need renewing after a few wettings.

It is a good idea to run an eye over what professional longliners use in the way of hooks. A firm that caters for professional requirements in this field lists the virtues of a longliner's hook as follows: a relatively long shank to facilitate removal of fish and baiting-up; a wide gape so that a large bait (e.g. mussel) can be held in the bend of the hook; a long, needle-sharp point with a small barb so that fish cannot

FIG. 9. Longliner's hook: note needle-sharp 'S' shaped point.

twist themselves free. These particular hooks are heavily galvanised and they are snecked, that is to say their points are off-set. Experiment shows that they are excellent hooks for angling and the special 'S' shaped point hones to optimum sharpness. In my opinion, hooks of this or similar design are a distinct advance over most of the familiar styles.

Float Fishing

Float fishing is a technique used in sea fishing usually when it is desired to fish a bait above rocky ground such as in gulleys for wrasse and bass or when mullet fishing. Mullet are dealt with later; however it can be said that they demand the nearest the sea-angler ever gets to the delicate float techniques of the freshwater fisherman. Most float fishing however calls for sturdy, easily visible floats. Fluoro orange is the most visible colour. Of the various float designs I prefer the elongated egg-shaped pattern with a tube through the middle to accommodate the line. The line is stopped at the most effective depth by means of a bit of rubber band secured by a Clove Hitch. This permits ready adjustment up or down as required.

The terminal rig for float fishing is very simple and consists of no more than a suitable weight such as a small drilled bullet together with a hook. If the bait is to be live prawn or ragworm I think there is a case to be argued for using a short-shanked hook both to reduce weight and thus permit the bait more mobility and to make the presentation look as natural as possible. A $\frac{1}{4}$-ounce bullet is usually about right for most locations. Having enough weight for casting this presents no problems since the float itself supplies plenty.

Float fishing in estuaries is a useful way of offering a bait when fishing over crab-infested ground. Indeed so profuse are shore-crabs in some places that this may be the only practicable way of fishing a bait. I well remember a party of Midland anglers who camped by the crab-haunted waters of an estuary and fished it expertly with heavy float tackle and accounted for a sizeable bag of flounders and school bass.

Some River Authorities controlling game-fish rivers and their estuaries enforce by-laws forbidding the use of float tackle. The idea behind this is to prevent the wholesale destruction of salmon and sea-trout parr by people trotting maggots down ground-baited pools. Whether these regulations would be applied in tidal reaches where sea fish are the quarry depends largely on whether the bailiff is convinced by the angler's explanation and his catch.

Rigs for Flatfish

The estuary angler, if he likes catching flatfish, will sooner or later feel the need for a special rig to suit these fish. There is no doubt that flatfish are attracted by movement of the bait although why this should be so is pretty obscure. The technique of drawing one's baited hook slowly over the bottom undoubtedly catches more fish than when the bait is left to lie static. Various rigs over the years have been devised with this thought in mind. It is often asserted that gaudy beads threaded on the trace above the hook act as an attractor for flats. Experiment suggests that this is true; but it seems to be just as true with various other species. All one can say is that fish are curious and tend to investigate anything that looks unusual.

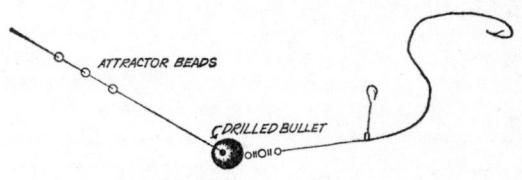

FIG. 10. Rolling two-hook rig.

Simple rigs are better than more complicated ones; and they have the advantage that they can be made up at the waterside. A rolling two-hook leger is particularly effective with flats when the estuary has a bottom of sand or firm mud. A $\frac{1}{4}$-ounce or $\frac{1}{2}$-ounce drilled bullet is threaded up the main line and retained by means of a swivel tied to the end of the line. The trace consists of a yard length of line ending in a suitable long-shanked hook. Eighteen inches above this hook a Blood Loop Bight is tied into the trace and a short snood is then attached to it carrying a second hook. The angler can experiment with beads and other attractors as he fancies.

This rig is fished by casting it square across the tide. The whole point is that the lead should be light enough to roll slowly in the current. Thus the angler fishes in a series of arcs. He should move position frequently and fish fresh water. This technique is certainly superior to static bait presentation and it works with both flounders and plaice. Obviously, you need a snag-free bottom to use the method and this means checking the area at low tide with an eye open for buried branches and other tackle-collectors. It is also, incidentally, a deadly way of catching salmon in low water using worm-bunch.

To use the technique effectively you really need to know the comparative speeds of the ebbing and flowing tides in the area you fish. On neap tides, especially in the early stages, very light leads may be used. On springs it may be correct to go as large as 2 ounces. The idea is to keep the bait moving in an arc as slowly as possible. When it pauses a tightening of the line against the current should get it on the move again, rolling and exploring its way over the bottom and taking the baits with it. Thus you are literally testing every foot of the bottom in a series of sweeps for fish which would be otherwise ignorant of the baits awaiting their attention.

Of recent years it has become fashionable to use flowing traces of quite inordinate length. In a recent article I found the writer advocating a flowing trace no less than 18 feet long. In my view this trend can easily become illogical and absurd. The virtue of the long flowing trace—especially when used from a boat—is that the bait is presented to the fish in a natural manner, being moved about freely by the tide. However it is also true that the angler becomes out of touch with his bait if the trace is excessively long. It is entirely possible for fish to gorge such a bait and move a few feet away before lying doggo. The surprised angler only learns about the event when he reels in to find why his tackle is producing no action. These tactics, in my opinion, are not very intelligent.

Very long flowing traces fished below static leger-weights are not for me. If I want to present a bait in a completely natural fashion I would sooner go the whole hog and rig up a drift-line. In that case, of course, the small lead is not in contact with the bottom. But at least there is no chance of a fish taking the bait and falling asleep.

Even drift-lining, however, does not eliminate all the problems because an angle tends to form between bait, lead and rod which again puts you out of direct contact with the fish. The effect however is a minor one and indeed there is a certain advantage in that fish do not instantly feel pressure from the rod when they touch the bait. Fish will, of course, sometimes hook themselves but whenever this lack of direct contact occurs in fishing the best remedy is for the angler to hold his rod at all times so that he can strike at the first suspicion of a take.

Materials

Before concluding this section on terminal rigs it would be a good idea to mention the raw materials in use. Saltwater fishing is devastating to all steel and iron products no matter how well they are protected. For this reason I insist on swivels and snap-links made of chromed brass wire. Excellently designed links in this material can now be obtained which are a vast improvement on the clumsy buckles and corkscrew links of the Edwardian sea fisher. In fact if the angler is prepared to produce a bit of wire work of his own to suit special occasions his purchases can be restricted to the quality swivels and snaps mentioned above.

Specialised terminal rigs such as wire traces have been left out of the present discussion which is aimed at estuary fishing. Wire is usually used for tope, shark and conger fishing. Although tope and shark do sometimes follow the mackerel into the mouths of large estuaries and conger penetrate some miles inland, these species are seldom sought specifically in estuarial waters.

Most anglers will want to try their hand at making leads in

the 3–5-ounce range as described earlier. These leads, supplemented by the purchase of a few 'Breakaway' leads and some drilled bullets in various sizes, will meet the needs of most situations. A small roll of lead sheeting from a builder's merchant will provide enough material to make fold-over leads for several seasons.

BREAKAWAY LEAD IN CASTING POSITION

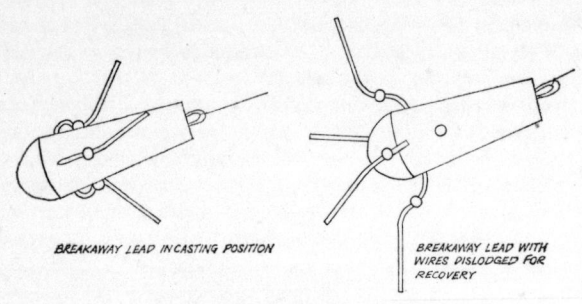

BREAKAWAY LEAD WITH WIRES DISLODGED FOR RECOVERY

FIG. 11. Breakaway lead.

One often sees spiral or Jardine leads offered for sale as sea-fishing tackle and, indeed, some angling books advocate the use of such leads. It should be remembered that they were designed for freshwater fishing and the wire running through the core and protruding at each end is usually steel wire. It will quickly rust away after a few wettings in the sea. Unless you can obtain Jardine leads made with brass wire the pattern is better avoided.

Among other specialised leads which may be usefully purchased are the pyramid-shaped 'Capta' leads which make good static leads for boat fishing. Their peculiar shape, when acted on by the tide, tends to press them to the sea-bed so that rather light weights may be used which are similar in holding efficiency to heavier ones. Heavy brass swivels are already cast into one of the faces of these leads to act as an anchorage point.

The knots to use when constructing terminal rings are quite straightforward and are all based on the Blood Knot and its many variations. Blood Knots are valuable for securing monofil because they avoid quick changes in angle and thus avoid self-cutting. Moreover, the coils tend to lock together and become slip-proof. Almost everyone knows the

Four Turn Half Blood which is used for tying a hook to a line. This together with the Three Turn Blood Knot for joining two lines and the Blood Bight for forming a slip-proof loop in monofil are really the only knots the beginner needs to learn.

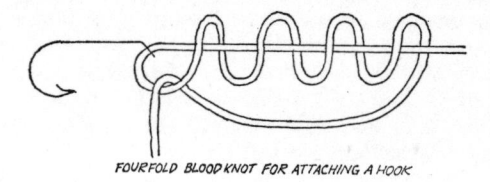

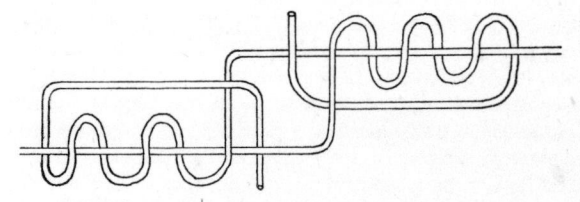

FOURFOLD BLOOD KNOT FOR ATTACHING A HOOK

THREE FOLD BLOOD KNOT FOR JOINING TWO LINES OF SIMILAR THICKNESS

FIG. 12. Blood Knots.

The thickness of the monofil used for terminal rings depends on how you are deploying the tackle. Techniques such as float fishing and drift-lining hardly call for anything stronger than 12-lb. line. For general ground fishing 15–18lb. line is a reasonable compromise. However, if you are shore fishing and intend casting your tackle long distances using a main line and collar as described earlier it is important to appreciate that the terminal tackle extending as far as the lead must be of a strength equal to the collar. Otherwise there is no point in using a collar and a break will occur due to casting-shock where the weaker line takes over. Snoods or traces below the lead may be usefully made of less robust material.

Sea fish in general don't seem to be put off by thick monofil in the way that freshwater fish are put off. The reason probably lies in the fact that most sea fish have never before seen a bait on a hook. Why not therefore use fairly heavy line on all occasions? Apart from obvious exceptions, such as float-fishing for mullet, there is no obvious reason why not. Certainly I have never heard a convincing argument that the use of small diameter lines really improves catches of sea fish.

The matter really hinges on sport and aesthetics. Recent attempts by certain tackle firms to make the sea-angler 'line-strength conscious' exemplify the trend. Light line competitions have been organised in which fish are sought using line of various maximum breaking strains calibrated to various species. The argument here, of course, is that it takes greater skill to land, say, a big bass on a 10-lb. line than it does on a 20-lb. line. This is true enough although it is also true that the trend could go too far.

Sea fish, generally speaking, are much more robust than their freshwater counterparts. And the point at which a light, sporting line becomes a foolishly weak one is often arguable. Strong lines are used in the sea, not particularly to overcome fish but to withstand the wear and tear of sand, shingle, seaweed and the drag of powerful currents. Unless the angler uses tackle appropriate to the particular situation he has lost touch with the reality of the sport and is really no better than the hunter who wounds deer at 100 yards with a ·22 rifle in the belief that such an unsuitable weapon is 'sporting'. A sea fish escaping with yards of thin nylon wrapped around its head and a hook in its maw may not present such an emotive spectacle as a wounded deer; but from nature's point of view there is little difference.

Baits—Natural and Artificial

Natural baits

Collecting natural baits is almost as interesting as fishing—as many anglers have already discovered. Men are simply grown-up boys and, although paddling around on a beach for fun is considered unseemly for adults, it is a perfectly proper occupation when it is described as 'bait collecting'. Because this makes it sound like a chore. However anglers often become so absorbed in getting bait that they miss the tide and can't fish with the bait they have found. This has happened to me more than once.

Some stretches of the British shoreline are almost barren of bait. Others have a prolific quantity of a single sort. Others again have such a wide variety that it is possible to collect a dozen sorts of bait in a hundred yard stretch. Some baits are very localised, for example, the Slipper Limpet. Others, such as Razor-fish, occur only in widely separated pockets.

Barren shorelines are nearly always composed of steep-to shingle banks with few sand-patches and rocks in which organisms can shelter. However you can also get barren sandy shores—and there is nothing 'deader' from the bait point of view than pure sand unrelieved by any trace of alluvial mud. Fortunately the estuary fisher seldom encounters these extremes. It is a feature of estuaries that they almost invariably always mix alluvial muds with their sands. These form rich beds in which the most popular of all sea-fishing baits, the marine worms, find suitable sanctuary.

Lug is the best-known of the marine bait-worms and it is likely to be found wherever sands and alluvial muds lie in an admixture. Almost every estuary has at least one lug-bed. Many estuaries have vast lug-beds in their lower reaches—a fact appreciated by fishermen for miles around.

Practically speaking, there are two sorts of lug of interest to the fisherman—the red and the black. Red lug is a good deal softer in the body than is black lug and it soon becomes a shapeless mess when it has been a few minutes on the hook. However, for many sorts of fish, I prefer red lug to black. The reason is that the softer bait exudes quantities of liquid into the water which acts as a great attractor of fish. It follows that you need more red lug than you do black for a similar period of fishing, the bait having to be changed more frequently. There is no better bait for bass, whiting and codling than a couple of red lug hooked once through the body.

Some anglers have a fetish for threading worms up the shank of the hook. This is a mistake with red lug. They should be hooked once, a third of the way down from the head. This permits the natural juices to leach slowly from the holes made by the hook and makes them more attractive for much longer. It is true that the tail of the worm will soon be nipped off by a fish; but it also true that this fish, having once determined that the worm is very edible, will not pause until it has swallowed the remainder, including the hook. Freshwater anglers have long been aware that the best way to fish worm is to hook it once only (or perhaps twice using a Stewart tackle) but sea-anglers, for no good reason, still mainly follow the traditional drill of threading their worms and rapidly squandering the coelomic fluid which is so attractive to fish.

Black lug is a thicker and altogether tougher bait than red lug and, for this reason, it is the sort one usually buys at the tackle-shops. It stays on the hook much better for surf-casting than does the softer bait which is why many anglers prefer it. For surf-casting it is advisable to thread the bait for half its length leaving half to dangle and act as an attractor and a reservoir for the liquids inside. Many anglers seem determined to get rid of these juices as quickly as possible and fish with what is literally an empty skin. When the fish show little interest the angler often complains about lack of action. It would be better if he condemned his own lack of know-how.

Black and red lug may be found together in the same bed. As a rule however black lug prefers a drier and more compact sand/mud admixture than does red lug. The worms are best obtained by digging using a flat-tined potato-fork in the case of the red and a narrow-bladed trenching spade for the black since these tend to burrow deeper than the other variety.

The lugs are only a fraction of the diverse worm-life to be encountered in a good bait-bed. The angler may well come across various sorts of ribbon worms, some species being very muscular and active. If flat stones abound over sandy mud it is worth turning a few over in search of a Bootlace Worm. Although thin, these creatures are enormously long. The largest I ever found measured 20 feet. Portions of such worms make excellent bait for mullet when float-fishing and for flatfish.

Some anglers make a special effort to obtain a few King-rag either by buying them at the shop, where they are not cheap, or by digging them in the stony estuarial muds they favour. They are superb worms, sometimes as thick as one's finger and coloured emerald green shot with purple, usually with a lighter underside. They range from about a foot to, exceptionally, as much as a yard in length. They have a pair of horny jaws and have the alarming habit of nipping the angler who handles them unwarily. Much of their attraction lies in their mobility in contrast to the lugs which attract largely by the bleeding of their secretions.

There are numerous species of smaller rags and the knowing bait-collector seeks these in the muds of backwaters and tidal creeks. Collecting them is a filthy task in the black alluvial muck but many fishermen consider them so attractive to fish that they will use nothing else. A good rag bed quickly yields an acceptable amount of bait.

Some worms are brought ashore by the tides, the most important being the Sea Mouse if one views it from the angling viewpoint. It is often washed out of the sand at the lowest part of the beach uncovered by spring tides. They are largish creatures being up to 4 inches long and an inch wide. They are reputed to be a good bass bait although I have never used them personally, perhaps because I could never quite figure out how one should put them on a hook.

Sea-anglers, like fishes, have got to adapt themselves to what is available as bait. Some estuaries have enormous amounts of one sort of feed while others feature things that are quite different. For instance if an estuary contains quantities of, say, baby shellfish then be sure that sea fish will be used to foraging for these items and will accept shellfish on the hook with great readiness. Experiment may show however that some quite different bait-form is attractive simply because it *is* different. Nevertheless, on the whole, it pays to conform to what the estuary produces naturally.

The unusual should not be overlooked. I used to fish some rocks at the mouth of a sandy cove both by night and by day. One evening I left a torch switched on by mistake on a rocky shelf only to find the whole area seething with activity. Literally scores of big sea slaters were scurrying around in the dark. These crustaceans are sometimes well over an inch long and they make an excellent bait for many sorts of fish.

Sandy bays near the mouth of an estuary often contain quantities of sand-eels. These active little silvery fish are one of the best baits in the sea. Being very prolific they bulk large in the diet of big plaice, bass, pollack and many other species. Some bait-suppliers now stock preserved sand-eels in plastic bags but these are a poorish substitute for fresh bait. When the sea is turbid the live eels can be caught with a prawning-net if the inside of the net is well-decked with seaweed; otherwise they will escape through the meshes. Some anglers collect eels with an eel-hook made up from scrap-iron by stroking the tool through the loose sand at the sea's edge where the sand-eels burrow. The exposed eel must be seized instantly because they can burrow out of sight in about half a second. The complete answer to eel-catching is to use a roll of fine-mesh seine netting.

The launce or Greater Sand-eel is a fish of the deeper water and is found in estuaries only at the seaward end. They are twice the size of the inshore sand-eel and may reach a length of over a foot. They seem to be a more free-swimming species than the lesser sand-eel and they are often encountered in mid-water. These fish form the main diet-item of many predatory fish around Britain's coats during the summer, especially large flatfishes such as the brill and turbot; large bass; pollack; ling and many more. The importance of the launce as a bait at the entrance to estuaries can hardly be over-estimated. They make an excellent dead-bait or can be simulated by artificials. When fishing live-bait most anglers use the lesser sand-eel which is easier to obtain and to deploy alive.

The only practicable way of getting launce is to fish for them. They will often seize ordinary mackerel feathers but better results will be experienced if a set of smaller feathers are tied for the specific purpose of catching launce. However, since they range far and wide in the tides, they are not always caught when needed. A substitute used by thousands of sea fishers is a thin strip cut from a mackerel. Whatever the method used it important to remember that the launce is a major bait-species in British seas during the summer months.

Crab is another familiar and popular bait for estuary fishing. The dark green shore crab is the form most usually encountered by the estuary bait-collector. It thrives below stones and wet seaweed hanging from rocks at the mouths of most sea inlets. As a bait for bass there is nothing to beat crab and it is equalled only by the launce. Crabs measuring about 2 inches across the shell are probably the handiest size for fishing purposes.

Quite a cult has grown up around crab as a bait since the war which can only be compared to some of the cults in flyfishing. Crabs shed their hard shells periodically as they grow bigger. A crab on the point of shedding is called a 'peeler' whereas one that has already shed its shell and is waiting for its skin to harden into a new shell is called a 'softback'. The crab cult hinges on these facts. For it is widely and frequently reported—with no evidence to support the claim—that peelers and softbacks make the best bait. Why this should be so is never explained. Peelers and softbacks, being almost defenceless, seek the most secure shelter possible and commonly burrow deep under large stones. In these hidey holes they can't be reached by predatory fish. Therefore they can form but a small and largely accidental part of a fish's diet. The truth is that, although fish do feed avidly on crab, it is not the jellified remains of softbacks we find in autopsies but the shells of hardbacks.

The main problem with hardbacks is getting them to stay securely on the hook, not a reluctance of fish to feed on them. They must be bound to a treble hook with elastic thread. If it is desired to cast crab a long distance I use what I call a 'crab-board' which is simply an oval bit of plywood with a hole bored through it to take the line. A crab is bound to each side of the board with elastic thread so that they are face to face so to speak. The line is threaded through the board, a treble is attached and one point of the treble is firmly lodged in the forward edge of the board. The board should be slightly wider than the crabs being used and a few nicks in the edge give the elastic something to grip.

It is widely assumed that sea fish must always be offered soft, tasty baits whereas a moment's reflection would show that if fish did, in fact, rely on discovering the large quantities of food they need in this form they would soon become very hungry. Fish in fact consume their prey as it comes, shells, protective armour and all and leave their jaws and intestines to ponder the problems of elimination. Anglers shell and prepare baits largely for their own convenience in getting them to stay on the hook and rarely experiment with other approaches. Baby mussels are a case in point.

CRAB BOARD UNBAITED

CRAB BOARD BAITED

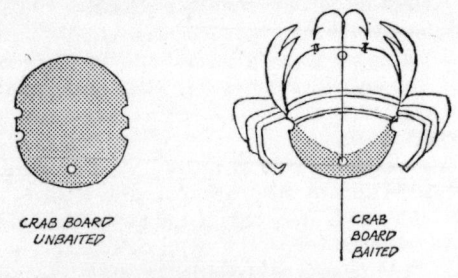

FIG. 13. Board for crab bait.

Having found so many young mussels in the stomachs of fish I tried the idea of hooking several of these small shellfish through the hinges of their shells and fished them in this manner. School bass and flounders took the bait without hesitation. The experiment was extended to cockles and Banded Wedge and proved equally successful. The value of this method of presentation lies in the fact that the creatures within the shells—even though the shells may be crushed or agape—are to a certain extent protected from the pecking of small pouting and other fry and remain so until a fish comes along sizeable enough to swallow the bait whole.

Obviously there comes a point where such reasoning loses its force and this is usually when cockles, mussels and so on are about half-grown. After this, they make better bait when they have been shelled. Large mussels, when shelled, make an excellent bait especially if they are a component of a 'cocktail'. Shelled mussel is a very soft bait and attempts to toughen it by salting, drying and so forth reduce its effectiveness as an attractor of fish. As with worm, this attraction is produced by the juices within the shellfish which salting and drying seem to destroy.

The idea behind 'cocktails' is to sandwich the soft shellfish between two layers of a much tougher bait such as squid, black lug or mackerel. If anglers used a bit more care when preparing such baits I am sure they'd get better results. After opening the mussel, for instance, the contents of the shell should be poured over the tougher items of the 'cocktail' when it will greatly improve their attractive properties.

Another shellfish of value as a bait is the cockle. Many estuaries have a cockle-bed and the molluscs can either be picked up by hand at low water or they can be scraped together using a long-tined rake. They tend to lie just beneath the surface of wet sand especially where freshwater flows. Flounders are particularly fond of cockle. I have never had bass on cockle.

Sometimes the Spiney Cockle or Rednose is encountered. These are twice the size of the common cockles and their remarkable scarlet 'feet' make them a sizeable bait for many species. To see a troupe of Spiney Cockles 'walking' towards the sea by levering against the sand is one of the most amazing sights of the seashore. My own experience with this bait however is disappointing and for this reason I prefer the common cockle for bait purposes.

A prime shellfish bait on the coasts I fish is the razorfish. These largish molluscs like quiet muddy bays in which to establish their colonies which are sometimes immensely prolific. The angler is interested in two forms of razorfish—the white and the brown. The white variety (*Ensis siliqua*) is the one most sought since it is the largest—up to 8 inches long—and provides succulent meat in quantity. The brown sort (*Ensis ensis*) is smaller and, in my opinion, is not quite so effective as a bait although I am unable to say why. Razor makes a first-class bait for all sea fish particularly bass, flatfish, cod and whiting.

Of the best-known methods of obtaining razorfish—with a razor-spear and using salt—it is largely a matter of what one wants to use the bait for that determines which of these is employed. The spear is certainly the quickest way of getting half a bucket of razor but the method does tend to tear the flesh of the bait. This matters little if the bait is to be used that day. However if you need a supply of undamaged bait to deep-freeze them for future use, as many anglers do, then the salt method is much to be preferred. Razorfish can also be dug with a spade but it is very hard work.

Spearing razorfish is not easy to describe verbally and it calls for a good deal of practice before the bait-collector becomes really proficient. The spear itself is a 3-foot length of $\frac{3}{16}$-inch diameter brass rod with a brass 'arrow-head' about $\frac{5}{8}$ inch wide soldered or brazed to its end. The rod should be carefully slit with a hacksaw in order to accommodate this arrow-head.

The mollusc signals its presence by spouting a jet of water from its key-hole shaped burrow and this means it is near the surface. It the spear is inserted into the burrow and worked very gently at different angles, using only the finger-tips, the collector is able to feel at which direction relative to the surface the burrow runs. In other words, a lack of resistance enables you to plot the tunnel where the mollusc is lying. When the right angle is discovered the spear is inserted smartly to its full depth when it should pierce the razor and bring it up, when recovered, on one of the barbs. The expert can collect razorfish almost as fast as he can pick them up using this method.

The salt technique which leaves the razors undamaged, works as follows: a plastic detergent bottle should be obtained of the type having soft sides and a narrow neck. This is cut in two about two-thirds of the way up from the bottom. Now charge the lower half by putting in half a cupful of salt and then fill it up with sea-water. Replace the top by sliding one half over the other and give the whole thing a good shake. The spout of the bottle (or a spout made from plastic tubing) is then entered into the mouth of the razor burrow and the bottle given a couple of squeezes, forcing brine down the hole. Remove the bottle and wait for the razorfish to emerge. This may be immediately or it may take a couple of minutes. Most anglers salt about a dozen holes and then back-track to pick up the emerged baits.

Frozen razor makes a reasonable bait and numbers of bass and other fish are caught on them every season. In preparing the razors for freezing they are shelled and laid to dry on sheets of paper. If they are air-dried in a warm breeze they must be protected from cats and rats which will be attracted from some distance. Salt sprinkled over the bait helps to toughen it. After this they can be placed, a dozen at a time, in small plastic bags and deep-frozen in the usual way. Although frozen razor is inferior to fresh bait it is nonetheless a very useful standby, especially in winter, when collecting bait is difficult.

Shrimp and prawns make an excellent bait and they are easy enough to collect at the mouths of pills and streams at low water. A folding prawn-net is handy for this job. These should be about 18 inches wide and have a collapsible head like a trout landing net and a telescopic handle. The usual prawn-nets are hopelessly clumsy and the folding net will need to be home-made. A useful alternative is to make a small drop-net. Drop-nets have the additional advantage that they will also capture hermit-crabs—a useful source of bait—as well as prawns. Prawns collect around seaweedy rocks at low tide in order to find cover from predators.

Artificial baits

As regards artificial baits we will first consider the case of the boat angler. Certainly he will want 'feathers'—that ubiquitous lure for catching mackerel, whiting, pollack and other fish. These are made with ease by whipping bucktail, plastic strips or hackles to a suitable hook. For general fishing I like to have two types—a white hackled, silver bodied lure of goodly size for dull sea conditions and a smaller, more sober lure for bright conditions and shallower water.

Feathers are usually spaced up the trace paternoster-fashion. Three are plenty to use at one time even when the object of the exercise is merely to obtain a quantity of mackerel for bait. If more than three feathers are used then some hooked fish will probably tear themselves free and this seems to me a repulsive way of fishing for sport.

Feathers can also be used from the shore and I have had many mackerel, pollack and other species by casting feathers from rocky venues fringing deep water using beach-casting gear and recovering the lures in a series of hauls on the dip-and-draw principle. You need at least 3 fathoms of water and no more than four ounces of lead to succeed at this game otherwise your tackle losses will become prohibitive. Considerable skill is needed in that the feathers must be brought

FIG. 14. Construction of simple feathers.

towards the surface progressively as the water becomes shallower and the weed-growth thickens.

Pirks, spinners and imitation eels

Pirks, spinners and imitation eels need to be considered as a group in order to make sense of the situation. It seems hard to believe that thirty or so years ago the only artificial lures used in sea-angling were the mackerel spinner and the rubber eel. In those days eels were made from rubber tubing mounted on a short length of wire which was cranked so that the bait tended to revolve. Alfred Powell writing in 1935 in the Lonsdale Library volume *Sea Fishing* begins to break away from this tradition by recommending flexible surgical rubber tube. However it was not until the 1950s, when soft plastics became available, that some attempt at representing a swimming, non-revolving, eel was tried. Some of these early plastic eels, oddly enough, were fair representations not of launce but of a swimming worm called the Paddleworm and they may have been successful on this count without the maker realising the fact. Whatever they looked like they caught fish and many a bass was lured to the writer's rod through their use. Later representations, such as the 'Red Gill', are a great advance on the old-style 'rubber eel' and show how problems of presentation can be overcome.

Every sea-angler who appreciates that the launce is paramount as a food-species in summer seas must wonder how best to simulate the slender creatures. One bass expert, who fishes offshore reefs by boat and claims to have had over 100 bass each over 10 lb., spent years working on experimental models of launce. He refuses to exhibit the result of this effort but it is reported to be a two-piece plastic eel about 8 inches long which is hard to detect from the real thing when it is in the sea. Whether this is so or not I don't know but it is certainly true that, for most anglers, the complete answer to launce-simulation has not yet been attained.

My own way with the artificial launce is to go back to rubber—but not the stiff tubing of yesteryear. I use a dense sponge-rubber of fine texture. The eel is cut from a $\frac{1}{2}$-inch thick sheet, the forepart of the body about $\frac{1}{4}$-inch wide tapering to a tail about half this thickness. A lateral curve is put

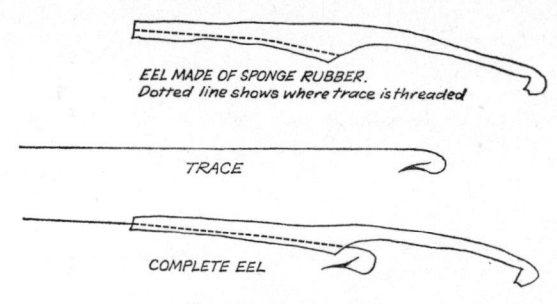

EEL MADE OF SPONGE RUBBER.
Dotted line shows where trace is threaded

TRACE

COMPLETE EEL

FIG. 15. Rubber eel.

into the tail during cutting. The depth of the tail is then reduced to about half using sharp scissors to produce additional flexibility and the head is made pointed like the real fish. A single hook is mounted on strong nylon which is worked through the body of the eel so the hook finally reposes midway under the belly and the nylon emerges from the nose. The finished product is then painted with matt colours—a careful selection of blues and yellowish-browns with a pale underside to resemble the actual creature. Tandem hooks improve the numbers of fish hooked.

The history of pirks really began in the U.S.A. where surf-casters found that a piece of metal, shaped to imitate the head of a small squid with soft tentacles attached, would catch fish. In Canada, Scandinavia and elsewhere it had long been known that anglers fishing through holes sawn in the ice could catch fish with flashing metal baits. Obvious deductions however were not drawn and anglers in Britain continued to use lug and similar baits for such predatory fish as big cod and whiting until very recent years. Yet an autopsy on the stomachs of these fish would have shown that fish is their main diet-item.

Pirks are easy to make. Chromed pipe about $\frac{1}{2}$ inch in diameter is sawn off in 3-, 4- and 6-inch lengths. A disc of wood or tin-plate with a $\frac{1}{16}$-inch hole through the centre is then used to blank off one end of the pipe. A piece of wire to fit the hole is inserted and held central with pliers while lead is poured into the open end enough to fill the pipe up to about a third of its depth. When cool, remove both disc and wire. One now has a pipe, leaded at one end, with a central hole. Some anglers complete the pirk by mounting a treble on stainless wire, passing the wire through the hole and packing the after-end of the lure with plastic car body-filler. However pirk fishing takes such a toll of baits I find it better to use a large single hook and to rig a device over the

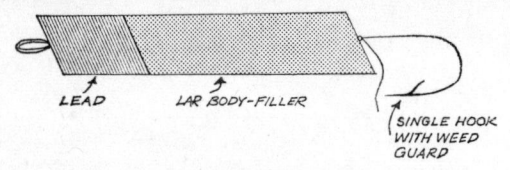

LEAD CAR BODY-FILLER SINGLE HOOK WITH WEED GUARD

Fig. 16. A home-made pirk.

bend to deflect weed. A great many pirks are lost by wreck fishermen and to avoid this it is best to tie the single hook to the lure with a line of fractionally less breaking strength than the tackle leading to the pirk. If caught up on the wreck you will then only lose hooks.

Pirks such as these are fished sink-and-draw from a boat where cod, ling, whiting and the like are known to congregate. In the bigger estuaries they work well in the deep channel as the tide flows and fish collect around known marks. The solidity of the lure and the direct contact maintained by the angler usually makes certain of very positive hooking.

Plugs are seldom discussed in reference to sea-angling no doubt because, as was the case with pirks, they still remain to be 'discovered'. Pollack, mackerel and bass will readily take a suitable plug in the right conditions. In summer when predators are feeding on brit and other fry a small plug fished in the surface layer can be quite deadly. Such fishing can be sea-angling at its best. A light spinning rod, fixed spool reel and 6 lb.-monofil line is the type of outfit to use for this work.

There is much room for experiment in the design of plugs for sea fishing. No one for instance, as far as I am aware, has ever produced a hollow plug which could be filled (or partly filled) with water in the manner of a bubble-float so that it has casting-weight while at the same time being buoyant. Bass and other fish can be very selective when feeding on brit which may be no more than an inch long and it is often useless to try and get them to take an artificial bait which may be three times that length. In these conditions a small plug drifted down to them so that it mingles with the brit is often quite effective. Balsa is a good material to use for these mini-plugs deployed on a drift-line and the result, in the best models, can be a quivering, incredibly life-like action.

Spin fishermen, whether from boat or shore, tend to rely on old favourites such as the 'German Sprat' which has taken thousands of bass off Splaugh Rocks in Ireland. Personally I am not very keen on these baits although I occasionally use them. The narrow spoons which Sweden produces in such excellent variety are also popular and very effective. However there is more to a spoon than stamping out a graceful-looking metal profile and putting a curve into it. It is my belief that spoons and other artificial baits induce takes not so much by their appearance as by the rhythm of vibrations they set up in the surrounding water. Thus some spoons fish well while others, although similar in appearance, fish badly. Only practical tests will determine which is the best fish-catcher. This of course is also an argument in favour of making one's own spoons in quantity and testing them out methodically in actual fishing.

Chromed brass rims from car headlights can be obtained from any scrap-yard. Using sharp tinsnips several long narrow spoons can be obtained from each rim. The profile is obtained from a photograph or is a carefully considered design of your own. It is drawn on thick cardboard, very carefully cut out and then the profile is stencilled on to the metal. The simplest way of making the spoon-blanks concave, when they have been cut out with tinsnips, is to make male and female dies out of hardwood, put the blank between the two, then draw them tight in a bench-vice. No two spoons will come out exactly the same and the only way of finding out which is the good, the bad and the ugly is to fish them. The majority will take a few fish in favourable conditions. Some you will stop using because they never seem to catch at all. One or two will nearly always catch fish although, in spite of the most careful weighing and measuring, you will be unable to discover why.

In view of the numerous experiments conducted on the design of artificial baits it seems surprising that there is so much to learn. An Irish professional fisherman, who had made thousands of baits of different sorts, told me that bronze has interesting qualities for bait-making. He believed this so strongly that he was prepared to saw up an old engine-bearing by hand in order to obtain the material. I am not prepared to scoff at this belief and it could turn out to be very sophisticated and scientific if it was fully understood. The fact is that we know very little about the sort of signal being picked up by a predator via the nerve-cells along its lateral line. It sems possible that baits having a certain resonance as they pass through the water could well have an attraction so far undescribed. After all, the alloy used in a bell is critical to the sort of sound it produces. It tickles the fancy to wonder what sort of effect you would get—no expense being spared—if a gold alloy was used. In fact I once heard of a man who used this very material while fishing at great depth in Lake Windemere for char and he had some good catches.

CHAPTER FIVE

Estuary Bass

Bass behaviour

Bass are particularly attracted to estuaries because these places act as natural food-traps. As with various other sea fishes they seem to have acquired a tolerance for freshwater even to the extent of being attracted to springs and outfalls of various sorts. It would be no surprise to me to hear that biologists had isolated a form of bass which was estuarine in nature just as they have isolated estuarine forms of trout. Research suggests that most individual bass spend most of their lives in and around a particular estuary and move out only for spawning and other special occasions.

Fishing for estuary bass calls for at least a superficial knowledge of the fish's habits and feeding patterns. A good way to study these is to take the cycle of a single tide. At low water you will often see bass—often big bass—lying in the brackish reaches of the bigger rivers. Observation suggests they are resting or, perhaps, 'socialising'. They often lie in rows—almost like huge sardines in a tin—with a dominant fish shoving the others over in order to gain a position in some favoured spot. There is an air of leisure and well-being about the proceedings and it is hard to believe they are not enjoying life. In such conditions they are not feeding and a variety of baits when presented for inspection produces no more than a bored rejection of the offering. Although the pundits prefer to interpret all this in terms of conditioned responses I prefer to think it is because the luncheon-gong worked by the tide has not yet sounded.

At the first lift of the tide these fish start to shift around with nervous movements, changing position in the communal 'bed' fairly rapidly. Soon first one then another drops back and begins to range around the pool before falling back still further and finally going to meet the incoming flow. After a few minutes the entire shoal has broken up and the feeding routine has now started. As the tide falls one can watch the whole thing in reverse. First one bass will appear and then another, cruising and milling around, until they finally start settling in their traditional lie. These lies, very often, are in the narrow pools beneath the arches of bridges because all fish, bass included, dislike the actinic effect of direct sunlight and seek the shadows.

Not all the stock of the river is like this, however, and a large proportion of the bass in the lower reaches do, in fact, move out on to adjacent coasts as the water drops. As the tide rises these fish appear to feed along the surf-line and round into the estuary-mouth from which they allow themselves to be carried inland. Feeding patterns are flexible although no doubt individual fish learn to adopt a productive routine which they repeat time after time. Certainly the first flush of water up many estuaries carries with it numbers of bass which are clearly well aware that the first fish on the scene is the one who gets the easy meal. Generally speaking this meal is crab because crabs that have spent the low-water period landlocked in pools and under seaweed can be caught without much trouble when the tide covers them. Bass will work in very shallow water picking up these morsels and it is no uncommon thing to see the waving tails of bass busy up-ending to reach crabs scuttling among the stones. I fancy that stranded crabs may suffer from a lack of oxygen and thus tend to throw caution to the winds when the tide comes in. Needless to say, there is no nonsense here about fish selecting peelers and softbacks. If a crab becomes visible it is likely to be snapped up no matter how its moulting process is faring.

Like many fish, bass are pretty catholic feeders and if rubbish is available quite a lot of them will make use of the fact. Sewers and outfalls do tend to attract bass—often fish of specimen proportions. Because of this trait I prefer to catch bass for the table from the lower end of estuaries or from estuaries that are not too badly polluted. This reaction is probably irrational because it can be fairly argued that once materials have undergone biochemical transformation they are entirely pure. Excellent vegetables, for instance, are grown on sewage compost so obviously this must be true. Indeed it is probably true also that bass and other fish, by feeding on wastes, are doing a good job in converting rubbish into protein.

Fishing from the boat

The bass angler, planning his tactics on a given estuary, will come into one of several categories. He will be fishing from a boat or from the shore. If from a boat he will be concentrating on deep water towards the estuary-mouth or be somewhere upstream. A boat undoubtedly furnishes a greater degree of mobility than any other method and better catches are the result. Moreover, a boat permits the use of either fresh or artificial sand-eel, possibly the deadliest bass-bait of all. Therefore we had better consider this technique first.

Although they are mainly a fish of the open sea, the launce often comes into deep water on a flood tide at the estuary-mouth. The lesser sand-eel, from which it differs only in size, is often found on sand-banks for some distance inland. Having collected a supply of eels at low tide and put them in a perforated container towed behind the boat to keep them alive, the angler heads for a likely spot in the tidal channel and, after dropping anchor, waits for the tide to lift. As soon as it does so an eel is baited by threading a hook into its mouth and out through a gill and the point very lightly nicked into the belly. The bait is then paid out on a drift-line using the minimum amount of lead needed to keep it well sunk. When a fish takes the bait it should be allowed to run, the line merely being tightened, when it will hook itself.

Trolling with an artificial launce is more active, covers much more water and is more skilful than might appear. There are various ways of deploying these eels and much depends on whether the eel is designed to spin or not to spin. Many modern eels of soft plastic do not spin and in fact some are lightly keeled with lead to prevent spinning. With non-spinning eels it is advisable to use an anti-kink lead to prevent rotation. This lead should be clenched to the line as far from the lure as possible taking into account the length of the rod in use. If eels with leaded keels need additional lead, as they may do in a strong tide, it can be added in the form of a swivelled bomb. The bomb is run up the line as high as the angler wishes—I like the weight to be 25 feet from the bait—at which point it is prevented from running back or 'stopped' with a bit of rubber clove-hitched to the line. The same leading technique is used with live sand-eel.

Much of the skill in trolling is boating skill allied with a knowledge of currents, where the fish are likely to be, and how the boat must be positioned in order to display the eel successfully. Too heavy a lead or too slow a trolling speed will result in fouling the bottom. This may go unnoticed when running over clean sand, the eel becoming snagged when the boat is over foul ground. If in doubt use a slightly lighter lead. The handling of the boat itself in relation to the set of different currents can only be learned by experience and nobody's experience is identical with that of another. The technique described below relates to a 15-foot bassboat powered by a 6-horse-power motor.

Assuming you have dropped down-river on the last of the ebb, you will be able to troll your eel across the lower pools just as the tide starts to lift. Slow, steady trolling is recommended and the weight of the lead adjusted as necessary. Cruise to and fro across the river so as to cross the lines of incoming fish. Pay out an adequate length of line—say between 50–70 yards. This is important because bass don't like the propellers of boats. Work the boat systematically and make your turns in wide sweeps so that slack line between rod and bait is avoided. Move progressively upstream, crossing and recrossing the channel and sooner or later a take is a certainty provided the bait is working right. As the estuary starts to fill it pays to extend the traverse even though one is then moving into shallow water and the boat will have to be speeded up to raise the eel. Bass will now be over these shallows looking for crabs but they will not refuse an eel trolled slowly past their noses. Eventually, experience will teach the right speed, the right spots and the right state of tide to make a catch that will raise many shore-fishers' eyebrows.

On some broad estuaries you will encounter a situation leading to what many experienced fishermen think is one of the most exciting prospects in British sea-angling. In high summer the vast shoals of brit, mackerel fry and other tiny sea-creatures become ever more tightly packed as they are attacked by predators. These may be mackerel, pollack, coalfish, large flats such as brill and turbot with even congers joining in the hunt. This activity attracts bass and the frenzied tiny fish, trying to escape, surge towards the surface. Here they lay themselves open to aerial attack from gulls, gannets and cormorants who have been sitting on the cliffs hoping for this very thing to occur. The bass fisherman too, who has been afloat from first light, a pair of binoculars glued to his eyes, hopes to join in the drama—but he is on the side of the tiny fish.

Actually the drama is more complicated than one first supposes. Although mackerel and school bass are intent on devouring as many brit as possible that is only the first stage in the proceedings. Really big bass and pollack are not interested in brit but in the lesser predators. To a 12-lb. bass a mackerel is just a snack. The activity is therefore at several levels and even larger fish such as tope start to show interest. It is probably the arrival of a really big predator such as a shark which brings these brit-massacres to an end as even the bigger fish scatter in panic and thus allow the remains of the brit-shoal to escape.

There are various ways of making use of such situations from the angling point of view. As mentioned, the first indication of the brit packing tight comes from the sea-birds. Exactly how they do it is not entirely clear. Observation suggests that they are attracted to a likely area long before brit actually appear on the surface. Bird behaviour is still a wide-open subject however and even such well-investigated instincts as migration still remain very puzzling. Smell may play a bigger role than is appreciated in that the great dense mass of brit exudes an oil similar to that given out by herrings and the birds may be able to detect it. An exception, I would suggest, is the gannet which seems to hunt purely by sight.

Gannets, indeed, are also a 'second stage' predator as distinct from the gulls, terns and puffins which are brit-feeders. When those splendid water-fowl the gannets begin their breath-taking diving this is a certain indication of fish and these fish will be either school bass or mackerel which of course are feeding on brit. So nature once again cunningly tips the scales in favour of the tiny defenceless fry. Diving gannets are a signal the alert angler can spot a couple of miles away and knowledge of what they are about obviates much searching of the sea.

An area of working bass is an incredible sight. The water is churned to white foam by the lashing of innumerable tails. Here and there the dark shoulders of fish will be seen lunging to and fro. The entire sea sparkles with the flashes of hundreds of thousands of minute fish shooting into the air and falling back. Scores or perhaps hundreds of sea-fowl whirl in a great circle picking up the dazed and injured. At close quarters such a sight is so primitive in its appeal that most people are quite fascinated.

The angler usually runs his boat uptide of such activity, cuts the engine and drifts through the area. Using a spinning rod he casts a lure over the feeding fish. Alternatively he can troll a bait round the fringes of the shoal. However, this is less satisfactory than drifting because, in spite of the frenzied activity taking place, a strong survival instinct still exists in predator and prey. Thus it is easy to alarm the fish and put the whole lot down. Whether the feeding is resumed deep underwater seems doubtful. Most likely the bass and brit scatter until the pattern duplicates itself at some other spot.

It will be noticed that I have tried to avoid over-use of the word 'shoal' when describing bass massed for attack on brit and small predators. In fact I don't think they are shoaling in the true sense of the word. Rather they are attracted to a particular area for a particular purpose and when the feeding is finished will disperse again to widely separated reefs and shorelines. The brit merely act as a temporary focal point.

What sort of artificial lures to use for bass in these conditions is arguable. Great execution has often been done with narrow spoons, German Sprats, Tobys and similar baits. But once it is appreciated that big bass are more likely to feed on mackerel and small pollack than on brit-sized lures then it will be seen that there is a need for something more robust. A mackerel split in two lengthwise with one of the halves mounted on a suitable tackle would not attract many schoolies but would certainly interest a better class of fish. The angler must decide what sort of sport he wants. It takes some determination to decline the use of a lure almost certain to give exciting fun in favour of a bait which may prove rather disappointing. If the bass-record is ever to nudge the 20 lb. mark in these conditions it may well come about by fishing a substantial bait as described.

Super-bass

A word might be said here about the size of bass. The record at the time of writing, 18 lb. 2 ounces, set up in 1943, was in fact broken by a 18½ pounder caught by a fisherman spinning in the Teifi estuary some years ago although, due to a misunderstanding, the record was not claimed by him. Bass of well over 20 lb. are reputed to have been caught in the Menai Straits on hand-lines. A 25-lb. or even 30-lb. bass, in my opinion, is not impossible although I doubt if such a fish will fall to the tactics usually adopted by bass fishermen.

Feeding and inshore movement

Like all living things, fish eat to live; their behaviour is modified accordingly. Whereas shoal bass or 'schoolies' are content with brit, lesser sand-eels, swimming crabs, shrimps and the like, bigger fish find the effort of hunting these small items in excess of their nutritional value. From the nutritional point of view the energy expended by a hypothetical 25-lb. bass searching for small food items exceeds what it is likely to obtain from those items. Other fish of course are in the same position. Research on trout, for instance, suggests that a distinct change of diet occurs when a certain size is reached. What this means is that fish move to feeding on a higher link in the food-chain so that they can obtain nutrient with minimum effort. Big bass are not really interested in the dainty items the average bass-angler uses for bait but are looking for fairly sizeable fish.

Why then do large bass turn up inshore as in the Teifi estuary and the Menai Straits? Invariably it will be found that a large amount of food is available in such areas perhaps due to special local conditions. In the case of the Teifi I believe an important factor is the presence of numerous salmon smolts, whitling sea-trout, small bass and mullet and the like. As for the Menai Straits—this is a curious place tidal-wise with a powerful current near the shore which produces deep eddies and backwaters. Big bass undoubtedly do get substantial pickings in such places although these locations are not typical. Most of the super-bass are found in the fast water around headlands and in the offshore overfalls where more sluggish species are largely at their mercy. However, from time to time they do enter estuaries, as explained, and the angler who hits one and is tackled for the occasion may find himself attached to the fish of a lifetime.

Scientific work on bass movements in the sea has produced some interesting results. Beginning in April, 1970, the National Bass Tagging Scheme was instituted by the Ministry of Agriculture and Fisheries. Some 959 bass were tagged with the help of nearly twenty different angling clubs. The results to date (1974) suggest that the smaller and younger fish, tagged mostly in estuaries and rivers, have tended to remain on home territory. Offshore fish tended to move around a little more even though, all things considered, they too were fairly static. Two fish tagged at Bude in Cornwall moved some distance—one ended up in the Hayle estuary and the other in South Wales. Of the 59 tagged fish captured to the beginning of 1973, 51 were caught by anglers, 7 by trawlers and 1 was taken in a salmon net. Bass are long-lived fish and since some hundreds of tagged bass are still not accounted for a final analysis is not yet possible. Any angler who does catch a tagged bass is requested to send details of the fish and where caught plus the tag to the Fisheries Laboratory, Lowestoft.

Not unexpectedly this report suggests that bass are creatures of habit with a fondness for their own estuaries. This is a good place to make a plea regarding conservation. Since the tagging experiment suggests that they are fish who like familiar haunts it is therefore entirely possible to fish a beach out by killing numbers of schoolies over and above any reasonable requirement. Anglers must act as active conservationists even though the impact they make in practical terms is modest. However it is only by thinking and acting as conservationists that any impact will be made on the real culprits. Some beaches I fish are swept by longshoremen using seines who are urged on by commercial firms advertising for such bass at something over 30p a lb. These sweeps along the shore should be illegal. They ruin beaches for weeks and it is a great disappointment to angling tourists—now a useful part of the economy in western areas—when they find the bass fishing poor due to the depredations of a few individuals. Conservation is still largely a word with the Ministry of Fisheries. Later, I will explain how inshore fishes could be conserved at very little cost.

Surf fishing

Many anglers like to fish for bass in the surf at the mouths of estuaries. This is low water work conducted on the last of the ebb and the early flood. An actual surf—as distinct from merely waves—is essential particularly if the weather is at all bright. This is the case even when fishing at night. Without a surf few bass will be found on an open beach.

Sea beaches vary due to their gradient and it is this factor, among others, which determines their composition. Flat beaches are usually of sand or fine gravel whereas steep-to beaches are generally of shingle, pebbles or rock terraces. All this is important to the bass fisherman because the gradient of a beach determines the nature of the surf. With flat beaches the waves break much further out than they do on steep beaches. In the former case this may mean wading with either thigh- or body-waders. This is because bass rarely enter shallow water in advance of the breaking waves largely because they feed on items washed out of the beach by the under-tow. As a general working rule it is reasonable to expect bass to be feeding in a moderate surf on a flat beach in water about 4 feet deep. This may easily be 100–150 yards from dry sand—hence the waders. Another working rule on a strange beach is to try and place the bait behind the second breaker as measured outwards from the shore.

Another factor enters the picture with surf-fishing and it is one the angler should treat with caution since it concerns his safety. Beaches open to the Atlantic are sometimes affected by surge. The cause of the phenomenon may have been a sub-tropical storm a thousand miles away. A long rhythm develops which is really a swell with a greatly extended amplitude. When this occurs it will be seen that the area of beach swept periodically is very large.

In these circumstances the wading angler must be most careful for it is quite possible to be standing on dry land one moment and to be waist-deep the next. The under-tow exerted by such long waves is enormous and quite enough to pluck the unwary off their feet. However, such a sea is a good bass sea since the water-tables between succeeding waves are much deeper than usual. In these circumstances the bass often advance in front of the first breaker to feed, proving that it is not the breaking waves that attract them but displacement of the beach produced by the under-tow. Much shorter casting than usual is recommended because the fish may be no more than a few yards from the dry sand and it is very easy to over-cast them.

If a strong lateral current is running I use a spiked lead such as a Breakaway with two short snoods on the trace above it, paternoster-fashion. The lowest of these hooks is on the sand with the second one about 18 inches above it. If there is little lateral current—as may be the case in some estuaries— I prefer either a Torpedo lead or a swivelled bomb. Being unspiked these tend to roll in what current there is and fish the baits in an arc. This rolling effect should be slow but unmistakable, the weight of lead being adjusted to suit. I am convinced that this presentation of the bait attracts fish which would not otherwise notice it. Indeed, it is no bad thing to carry your gear in a haversack and fish slowly along the beach almost like a wet fly fisherman. This is fairly hard work compared to the tripod, bell and seat one often sees but if the object of the exercise is to catch fish then the method is warmly endorsed.

Quite a lot of bass take by swimming forward on the wave, lifting the lead and slackening the line. Unless the rod is held by the angler these slack-line bites are impossible to detect until it is too late to strike. Brass bells attached to fishing rods help to lose hundreds of fish each season by giving a false sense of security because they only work if the fish jerks the rod and a great many do nothing of the sort. Slack-line bites are best dealt with by the angler running backwards up the beach until he feels the fish and then striking. The thrilling jag-jag on the rod followed by the bass heading seawards needs only for the angler to lean back holding the tackle and the honed hook will do its work. On a flat beach it is relatively easy to beach a bass with the help of the waves.

Crab is probably the best bait for surf-fishing at the mouth of estuaries closely followed by fresh razorfish. A thin lask of mackerel cut to the approximate length of a sand-eel is also good. Frozen razor and herring sometimes catch fish although they are not my first choice.

Up the estuary

With slight modifications these tactics can be used most of the way up an estuary. Anywhere where there are mudbanks and rock areas containing crabs are likely spots. The mouths of gulleys leading into the main channel are often prime locations; bass seek them out because they act as food-traps. Eventually, however, most estuaries tend to take on a lagoon-like appearance. Worm is well worth a trial here. By fishing really light and adopting what are practically freshwater tactics the angler can frequently enjoy sport with schoolies in large numbers even if a belief in the virtues of conservation makes him return all or most of his catch.

The middle and upper river is where the spin-angler comes into his own. It will be appreciated that most bass stream in and out with the tides and are therefore very mobile indeed. They do however tend to stick to certain runs or lines of travel so one needs to be pretty selective about choice of venue even when a boat is being used as a casting-platform. In these quieter, upper waters it pays to either anchor the boat or to drift. Running the engine will do nothing for the sport and may well ruin it.

As regards spinners for this work, I favour a self-weighted wobbling spoon about 2 inches long home-made from chromed brass. The Norwegians make excellent ones which can be bought in the shops. However, the weight must be precisely right for the rod in use—neither too light nor too heavy. Spoons that are not self-weighted—ones that need lead on the trace in order to make them heavy enough to cast —are not suitable for the light, balanced spinning we aim to achieve. Narrow leaf-shaped spoons are good since they simulate the fluttering of a small fish.

If one studies the river-channel at high and low water a place will be found where the fast incoming current suddenly spreads out due to sand-banks and other features and the estuary becomes temporarily wider and the water shallower. Any food items being swept along tend to get dropped as the current slackens. Bass are often found foraging in such spots and parts of the estuary where this effect occurs are well worth the spinner's attention.

Having found a suitable venue the shore angler can take a stance and fish both the flowing and the ebbing tide. There is little need to move around a lot in these conditions because there will be a constant passage of fish. Even so, it pays to keep an eye open for localised activity and to cash in on this should it occur. Shoals of school bass often hang around some restricted location—often the mouth of a small gulley—whereas the heavier fish seem to forage along the shore more systematically.

Bass are greatly attracted by warm water outfalls, largely because these harbour vast numbers of food species. One of the bass hot-spots in Milford Haven, for instance, is the point where the water from an oil-fired power station is returned to the cooler waters of the Haven. It is known that such artificially heated areas stimulate fish-growth, especially crustaceans and allied forms. A feature of some of these outfalls is a tide-deflector. Some experts feel that these deflectors tend to disorientate small fish by the turbulence they create and thus provide a non-stop supply of easy meals for bass. Typical of the fare eaten by such outfall bass is the following: pouting to $\frac{1}{2}$ lb., blennies, poor cod, small whiting, sprats and small flatfish. Outfall bass often show an interest in dead baits such as sprats, frozen and preserved sand-eels and lasks of mackerel. Spinners, too, will catch their quota of outfall fish. Easy fishing—and outfall fishing can at times be very easy—tends to attract greedy individuals. An outfall at one South Wales power station used to be plagued by people who threw pieces of metal covered in treble hooks across the tide with the deliberate intention of foul-hooking as many fish as possible. However, after several of these chaps had appeared in court the practice became less popular.

Whether bass are less prolific in our estuaries than was once the case is hard to say. Certainly it can be said that there are still large stocks of these powerful fish along the offshore reefs and the fry from these stocks probably tend to redress the losses resulting from the average bass mortality rate. If there are less fish than in late Victorian times the fact is not readily noticeable. Indeed, this season (1973) more double-figure bass have been recorded than ever before—some as far north as Scotland. The age of offshore oil-rigs around Britain however is only beginning and how the almost inevitable pollution will affect bass and other fish remains to be seen.

Fortunately bass do not easily fall victims to commercial

fishing. They are uncommonly caught in trawls although they can be seined from an open beach. The main offshore bass stocks live around rocky reefs which are difficult to approach by boat except on neaps and where trawling is almost impossible. Moreover the fish are such speedy travellers—moving miles on a single tide—that most commercial fishing methods are ineffective. This is lucky for the bass and for the angler and, if it were not so, the species would now be as rare as the haddock has become in southern waters.

Which method of catching bass gives the most satisfaction? On balance and all things considered I think probably live-baiting with sand-eel. The tackle is of the simplest consisting of no more than a light line, minimal lead and a hook. The angler is thus in intimate contact with his fish and can thus enjoy the maximum in sport that the bass affords. In my opinion this is estuary fishing at its best because very considerable skill needs to be acquired before the fisherman regularly starts to clobber bags of 4- and 5-pounders in the manner of the experts. To those who take the trouble to acquire the technique, I doubt if any other method gives such consistently good results taken over a season.

Many anglers are put off trying the method by what seems the difficulty of obtaining the live eels. On a strange estuary I agree that one can spend a fairly hard day making inquiries about the location of sand-eels and trying different spots. But once you know where to go and can obtain enough eels at the bottom of a spring tide to last you through a few hours fishing there is no looking back. They are, I am convinced, as near as one will ever get to the perfect bait.

CHAPTER SIX

Estuary Mullet

Kinds of mullet

This is a book on fishing, not on biology. Even so, it is necessary to discuss the various sorts of mullet in British waters so that we know what sort of fishes we mean by the term 'mullet'. The only mullets of interest to the estuary angler are what are called 'grey mullet'. These are subdivided into three sorts – the Thick-lipped grey mullet, which is the most widely distributed; the Thin-lipped grey mullet and the Golden or Long-finned grey mullet. The Red mullets, as far as I know, are not found in estuaries except as rarities.

The grey mullets are one of the most characteristic of estuary fishes. Many anglers, indeed, have never seen a mullet in the open sea and have certainly never caught one in that location. However, mullet do of course shoal in the open sea and are caught quite often with rod and line especially from beaches fringing sandy bays. Grey mullet tend to be a sub-tropical fish and, like bass, are most prolific along our south and south-west coasts. However, due to the variations of the North Atlantic Drift, they have been seen as far north as Bergen. Michael Kennedy reports Thick-lipped grey mullet as being 'common' in the Orkneys. I would query the word 'common' because a recent assessment of fishing in Lerwick Harbour in the Shetlands by Cavy Johnson reports that mullet are only 'rumoured' around Gremista and that 'mullet are uncommon in Shetland'.

It can be said therefore that mullet are fish which delight in warm, estuarial waters. They are found in quantity in sheltered waters from North Wales south to Jersey and from Cornwall to Poole, Portland and Dover. Margate used to be noted for its mullet as did Pagham Harbour in Sussex. A specimen Thin-lipped mullet of $16\frac{3}{4}$ lb. was netted in the latter and preserved by the British Sea Anglers' Society. However, the present record of 10 lb. 1 ounce for this species was caught at Portland.

One thing can be said at once about mullet – and that is that they are a very much under-rated species. As a fighting fish capable of long runs and sustained effort I would say they are almost as good as bass. In terms of the finesse required to catch them I'd rate them superior to bass. Yet only a relatively small number of anglers set out to catch mullet each season and those who have developed the know-how to make consistent catches possible are incredibly few in number. Why this is so I cannot imagine except to suggest that mullet have not yet become a 'fashionable' angling fish in terms of the publicity accorded certain other species. One would think that the mullet's reputation for being uncatchable would have enticed more fishermen to try their hand than is the case.

Mullet are not in fact uncatchable although they can admittedly be extremely difficult when approached in the wrong locations. Even Clive Gammon concedes that there are only two venues he knows where mullet can be caught in quantity. One of these will be discussed later in the light of the writer's experience. However, this tends to over-state the position and mullet are caught in many places and often in quantity although real angling skill, local knowledge and much trial-and-error will be needed before the stranger learns the secret of mullet hot-spots.

Feeding mullet

The mullet is largely a surface-feeder in the shallowest of estuary water. Obviously, feeding in such locations, it has learned to be a very cautious fish. It is a creature that drifts silently on the tide like, as someone put it, a 'grey ghost'. Instead of swallowing a bait it prefers to suck and taste— and anyone who has had dealing with shy-feeding roach of similar habit knows how infuriatingly difficult such fish are to hook. This sucking trait is so marked that such adjectives as 'impossible' and 'uncatchable' have been used by various anglers over the years whose abilities have hitherto been tested only on dogfish and other gross feeders.

One of the first things the would-be mullet fisher must study is the fish's diet. What do mullet eat? When do they eat? What bait should the fisherman use? These important points must be considered in detail if any sort of success is likely to be achieved.

That invaluable work *The Sea Angler's Fishes* by Michael Kennedy reports that mullet often nose around weed-covered rocks, the hulls of boats and the like. From this he concludes that they like sucking the green and brown algae found growing in these locations. Out of this, he thinks, they swallow a variety of tiny molluscs and crustaceans. Other diet items include an assortment of tiny bivalves and univalves, small marine worms and even the larvae of certain midges of marine habit. In many harbours, however, it is the floating offal which is the main attraction and, indeed, Kennedy quotes a case of ray carcases being scavenged by the fish. Perhaps more familiar is the presence of mullet around the ubiquitous harbour drains. Fish scraps from fish factories and edible refuse dumped from ships' galleys are another source of nutriment to mullet.

The gut of a mullet is almost like the gizzard of a bird and for this reason they need grit, the fine particles being retained and the coarser ones expelled. We thus have a species at much at home with decomposed animal and vegetable matter as it is with green weed, sand grains and insect larvae. Small wonder, perhaps, that some anglers find the mullet a difficult fish to lure to a bait.

Mullet feed on both the flooding and ebbing tide with exceptions to be noted below. Coming in on the flood they allow themselves to be carried along while they watch the surface and linger around any floating substance or object capable of being nibbled, tasted or sucked. It is while doing this that spectators see the heart-stopping swirls of big mullet and the speedy V-shaped wakes they slash in the surface on being slightly alarmed, perhaps by a passing bass. The whole surface of an inlet may be covered by these boils and surges so that even non-anglers stare with interest and wonder about having a try for the big fish. However, they little realise that they would be trying their hand against one of the most difficult of all common sea fish.

At one time or another I suppose just about every bait ever heard of has been tried against mullet. Everything, that is, from banana to tripe and from fish-guts to white ragworm. Mullet have a capacity for sucking and tasting such a wide range of substances that the choice of a hook-bait becomes a special problem. In the last resort the angler can only take his cues from what he deduces from his powers of observation.

One of the first things, rather obviously, is to examine carefully the surface of the water you intend fishing for mullet, especially on the ebb tide. Discover what is drifting to sea. Apart from the floating trash usual in estuaries there may be some particular substance coming from a particular location. It could be fish scraps from a jetty or stale buns thrown out of the hatch of a moored ship. If it is likely to be a regular feature of that bit of water then be sure the mullet shoals have become used to feeding on it and will take a bait composed of this substance far more readily than any of the many alternatives. Should you spot mullet busy feeding you can check up with binoculars on the cause of the activity or row over and collect a sample. It may be unspeakable goo or it may be a fairly solid substance which could point the way to possible hook-baits.

Tackle

As regards tackle, no strict rules can be laid down because mullet venues vary from a nice grassy bank beside a tidal pool to mile-wide estuaries complete with anchored ships, buoys and other obstacles where hooked fish have got to be held tight at all costs. I can only describe what I like to use for these fish. The rod needs to be reasonably long, light and of high quality tubular glass construction. A two-piece, spigot-jointed, glass blank with a fast action and a length of between 11–12 feet should prove to be about right for most anglers. To this should be fitted a fixed-spool reel loaded with 200 yards of 6-lb. line. As regards hooks—I use a size 8 or 10 freshwater hook which is discarded after one outing. A supply of leads in the form of shot and lead-wire will also be needed. For a float I generally use peacock quill with a length of about 8 inches.

In considering the tackle required for bait-fishing it would be a good point here to consider also the tackle for fly-fishing. In this connection it may surprise many anglers that mullet can, in fact, be caught on fly but this is correct. Fly has been particularly effective at, among other places, Durlston near Swanage where mullet up to 5 lb. have recently been taken by this method. When I occasionally fish fly for mullet and school bass—which also take fly avidly—I use a light, two-piece, 9-foot tubular glass fly-rod kept for this purpose. An inexpensive floating fly-line, a trout-size fly-reel and some 6-lb. monofil to cut into casts represents the rest of the gear. It is the sort of outfit you might assemble for trout fly-fishing almost anywhere. However, make sure you have plenty of terylene backing under the fly line because one day you may need every yard of it.

What do mullet take the fly to represent? There is no ready answer; nor do we really know why flounders pursue a big spoon. All that can be said is that they do. However, a clue may lie in the fact that Jersey mullet fishermen sometimes use ground-bait made up from immature shrimps which have been boiled and salted mixed with bread-crumbs. The hook-bait used with this mixture is a boiled, peeled shrimp. It is an interesting fact that whitish, shrimp-like flies about half an inch long are the most effective ones you can use when mullet fishing. One can only conclude that baby shrimps form a major part of the mullet's diet and it is these that the fly-fisher is simulating, albeit unwittingly.

Location and fishing methods

I said earlier that mullet feed on the flooding and ebbing tide. However they also feed in static tidal conditions when they are landlocked due to special circumstances. The landlocking effect may be due to the formation of saltwater lagoons and the like in which the fish have become trapped. A situation of this sort occurs when the natural ebb of the tide is held up by artificial means in order to activate machinery such as generators, water-mills and the like. Trapped in the salt lakes thus created mullet lose a good deal of their caution and feed much more freely. It was a venue of this sort—the tide-mill pool by Carew Castle in Pembrokeshire—which was referred to by Clive Gammon as one of the few places he knows where mullet can be caught in quantity.

Carew, indeed, is ideal for mullet fishing. Once the gates in the barrage close under the first pressure of the outgoing tide, the mullet are sealed into a steadily diminishing saltwater lake which never, however, runs entirely dry. No doubt this upsets their normal feeding pattern and, as the surface-area shrinks, they become steadily hungrier as the choice of food declines. Anglers in the area have known about this for generations and make their plans accordingly.

I fish this particular venue by timing my arrival to coincide with the last of the flood tide. Preferably this should be a spring tide so that plenty of fish have been brought up into the lake. Bait will have been obtained earlier, a favourite with me being small white ragworm. A fragment about an inch or so long is threaded on to the hook. Some anglers use paste and some good catches on this have been reported. The basis of the paste is bread with such ingredients as boiled fish, boiled cabbage and potato mashed into it. Cabbage boiled until it is really soft is also good for ground-baiting—as well it might be considering the mullet's fondness for vegetation. Some anglers pin their faith on floating crust, fishing it as if they were after carp and seem to do well on occasion.

Ground-baiting—strictly speaking, it is surface-baiting—certainly attracts and holds a shoal of mullet and, in this respect, they can almost be treated as if they were a shoal of rudd. In an enclosed lagoon such baiting is easy enough but in an open estuary, thanks to tidal currents, it may not be a very good plan. There is very little point in baiting if the tide is likely to change and lead the fish away from the angler. Bread, bran, boiled offal and so on can be used for groundbait. Prawns and shrimps, if they can be spared, make an excellent ground-bait if boiled and pulverised. In this case a dozen or two of the smallest should be retained, peeled, and used as the hook-bait. Fish-paste mixed with fresh bread is also said to be good on the hook.

The float is adjusted so that it fishes the bait about 2 feet deep. Some experiment may be needed here because mullet sometimes feed 4 or 5 feet deep in shallow water. If there are no mullet visible on the surface they could well be feeding below the surface although this is not usual. When they are present one almost always sees a telltale bulge or swirl of the water even if it is only an occasional one.

Some anglers prefer to dispense with a float and use a floating, leadless line instead. This is often possible in lagoons; another alternative is to use the fly outfit. A bubble-float can be employed as a casting-weight if it is desired to flick a bit of crust in the path of cruising mullet. One wonders if there is any soft bait these surprising fish will not take. Cereals are also worth a trial. They should be prepared as for coarse fishing and be included in the ground-bait, a single grain being deployed on the hook.

Mullet fishing calls for keen eyesight and instant responses. A fish will become interested in your bait and spend 10 minutes sucking and nibbling at it. If the water is clear you may catch a glimpse of your quarry as it plays around, pausing to suck at some other item on the surface, then returning to taste the bait on your hook. No other form of sea fishing that I have heard about calls for such concentration by the angler nor for such lightning reactions. Because, when you have lost all hope of an actual bite, your float, instead of merely dancing and bobbing in small circles, will instantaneously have shot out of sight. Possibly the mullet has sucked a bit too hard and pricked himself with the hook so that it has penetrated the skin of the lip. Or maybe he has drawn in some water and this has carried the hook with it into his mouth. In either case you have only a fraction of a second in which to tighten. Anglers who think they have a fast response to quick-biting roach are encouraged to try their hands with mullet. Many will find their reactions slower than they thought.

Opinions differ over the fighting qualities of mullet. Some anglers consider them a lot inferior to bass. The fact is that there is a good deal of variation in fish, both saltwater and fresh, not only regarding their sporting qualities but even their flavour on the table. I can only report that the mullet I have caught have given considerable fights, one of which is memorable even after a lapse of some 20 years.

The fish was hooked in a corner of Carew mill-pool after the usual 10 minutes or so of tantalising sucking at the bait. I tightened to find myself into what was obviously a good fish. At first I put it between 3–4 lb. in which time it was boring around a few yards from shore. Although I managed to turn its head a couple of times there was no sign of it tiring. A quarter of an hour later it was still going strong and had made a couple of boring runs which took it 50 yards out. In the end it made a final run and broke me clean, taking 100 yards of line with it. Maybe this was a foul-hooked fish although it didn't play like one. I put it at between 7–10 lb. and it was certainly the best mullet I've ever handled. No doubt it went down-river on the next tide. I hope it got rid of the hook.

The cream of sport with mullet, however, is to be had using the fly. And don't forget that if you have no trout fly-tackle available you can fish the fly using a spinning rod, fixed-spool reel and bubble-float. It isn't as much fun as using fly-tackle but it is very efficient and catches fish as well, if not better, than a conventional fly outfit. If you haven't tried the method, the idea is to half-fill the bubble-float with water and slide it up the line until it is about 4 feet above the flies. The flies can then be cast and retrieved over the surface with ease. Good flies to use are Teal-and-silver dressed on small hooks. Or one can try to dress a fly to simulate a baby shrimp. After being cast near feeding mullet the flies are recovered slowly with imperceptible jerks after the manner of a swimming crustacean.

This technique has been particularly effective from beaches around Swanage in recent seasons where it has accounted for mixed bags of bass and mullet. Wareham, Dorset, anglers who specialise in the method report spectacular battles with big fish not all of which are won. Even so, catches of up to two dozen fish on a single tide are not uncommon.

Fishing fly for mullet very much lends itself to use of a dinghy and oars. There are few more pleasant ways of spending a summer evening than to pull quietly round a harbour on the evening tide while dropping a fly beside flotsam being patrolled by mullet. Needless to say, it isn't all action. Mullet are very perceptive fish and they are very easily startled. They have no use for the waning sun glistening on a thick leader and the angler will find that the sport drops off if he uses monofil much thicker than about 6 lb. Mullet, indeed, seem to be the one exception to the rule mentioned earlier that the thickness of the line has little effect on sea fish captures. With mullet I'm sure it has a marked effect.

Mullet fishing usually starts in early summer. The first surface-feeding will be observed generally during the first warm spell in May. Kennedy reports that mullet disappear from the shallows in October and November although a lot depends on what sort of a season it is. This year I saw a good mullet taken from an open coast beach in mid-November as it headed for deeper water at the approach of winter. After a mild winter arrivals as early as mid-February have been noted. I have never tried autumn fishing for mullet although bumper catches are still made in Devon. Millbay Docks at Plymouth used to be noted for autumn mullet. Small mullet do not seem to be too worried by the cold and large shoals turn up along the south coast even in mid-winter when they are often scooped up in seine-nets.

Mullet have long been a target for the inshore netsman. Hauls of up to around 100,000 fish are on record, usually in the West Country. Kennedy claims there is a westerly migration towards the end of the year when vast shoals collect around Land's End in the Mount's Bay area. Seine-netters commonly trap shoals in a convenient pill by stretching a net across the mouth. The mullet's well-known habit of hopping over the head-rope of the net and thus escaping can be prevented by the traditional ruse of scattering straw on the water on the inside of the net to give the surface the illusion of solidity.

The Thin-lipped mullet adapts itself well to freshwater and the Thick-lipped species only marginally less so. I have noticed that mullet are in the habit of slipping quite a long way up salmon rivers in the autumn. They probably accompany migrating game fish. On the West Cleddau they are commonly seen a mile or two up into freshwater and on the Teifi have been reported four or five miles above the tide. It is possible that seals may chase some of them upstream although I think the floods of autumn have more to do with it. In my experience it is useless trying to catch mullet in freshwater since they appear not to feed once they leave brackish water.

Some estuaries and harbours attract mullet in shoals; yet others, although they appear equally suitable, seem to have few. Exactly why this should be so is rather a puzzle. Although they thrive in water short of oxygen and even where there is mild pollution, I doubt if these are factors. More likely the adjacent coast doesn't suit the species—perhaps by the fact that it is rock-bound or for some less obvious reason. Their ability to tolerate mild pollution and oxygen-shortage makes them a good subject for marine aquaria. This is largely because they have the ability to absorb oxygen by gulping mouthfuls of air which they pass over their gills.

As a culinary proposition I am not very attracted to estuary mullet although, admittedly, I have heard other opinions expressed—often by those expert with the use of herbs. In my opinion, however, if you need herbs before you can eat a fish it is better to forget it and enjoy the herbs. Much no doubt depends on what the mullet has been eating; rank offal is hardly likely to produce a delicate flavour. Mullet have rather oily flesh and baking seems to be the method most advocated by the experts. Surprisingly enough, however, frying—the first and last resort of the amateur cook—is also advocated, especially for small mullet.

Mullet are certainly under-rated. They present angling organisers with a great opportunity to explore the potential of what, to most anglers, is a strange and rather mysterious species. Speaking for myself, I would sooner fish free for 5-lb. mullet than pay £1 or more a day to catch herring-sized trout. However many do just that and then grumble about over-crowding. If a charge was made for the mullet fishing in estuaries no doubt there would be a rush to form clubs and disappointed applicants would be turned away by the hundred.

CHAPTER SEVEN

The Flatfishes

The flounder

Of all the flatfishes the most characteristic of estuaries is the flounder. Flounders delight in shallow water over mud or sandy mud and there are few places the species does not penetrate including all the pills and gutters reached by the tide. Moreover, they are as much at home in freshwater as in salt and have been observed over 40 miles from the sea. No one would seriously claim that the flounder was a sporting fish. Even so, flounders provide sport and food for thousands and many a sea contest has been won by the angler's skill in obtaining quantities of the fat flats to boost his score at the weigh-in.

The flounder has a thicker body and a larger head than its near-relative, the plaice. It also seems to suffer more from disease than plaice do—perhaps because of its freshwater visits. Normally, the eyes of flounders are found on the right side of the head although in some districts reversed examples occur. As regards size—a 3-lb. flounder can be considered a specimen. The biggest rod-caught flounder weighed 5 lb. 11 ounces which I think is near the maximum for the species even in rich feeding conditions. The professional flounder-netsmen on the Towy, which is an excellent feeding-ground, had not seen a flounder bigger than about 6 lb. when I asked them.

Flounders move in from the sea in spring. At this time they are out of condition and hardy worth catching. By May, as the inshore water begins to warm, they are improving in condition daily and are beginning to establish a pattern of moving in with the tide which they will maintain for the rest of the summer. In the autumn the reverse process takes place and where I often fish, in Carmarthen Bay, good flounder catches are made from the open shore in October and November as the fish abandon the estuaries and move out towards their spawning-grounds in the sea.

On our part of the coast a good flounder is between 1½ lb. and 2½ lb. in weight. Like all sea fishes they are opportunists and quickly adapt their diet to what is available. Small shore-crabs, sandhoppers, gobies, worms, herring fry, sand-shrimps and razorfish are typical of food devoured by flounders. They also have a great fondness for immature bivalves, especially cockles. Indeed, in our particular area, cockle is one of the best baits one can use. Small ragworms are also much appreciated by flounders who seem to be fascinated by the active movements of the creatures.

Many flounders are caught by anglers surf-casting for bass especially when a rolling leger is used. I have heard it said that flounders do not like a rough sea but this has not been my experience and one of our best bags—consisting of fish on or over the 2 lb. mark—was taken from a moderate surf in late September in Carmarthen Bay. It was noticed that fish in these conditions were feeding close to the shore, often in no more than a couple of feet of water. If spiked leads had been used in anchoring our tackles far out in the surf the baits would not have rolled round and picked up the flounders. These tactics have paid off on so many occasions that we now use them as standard routine when we want flounders.

It is always worth casting an eye on how professionals deal with particular fish. Large quantities of flounders are taken from various estuaries by the use of chicken-wire nets. The coil of wire is unrolled parallel with the water about two-thirds of the way down the beach. The wire is then supported in an upright position on stakes with a coil or scroll formed at each end facing up the beach. Wire about 4 feet deep is used for these flounder-traps. After the tide has flooded the traps it starts to turn and this is the signal for flounders to work their way back towards the centre-channel. On encountering the trap they make their way along it only to end up in the scroll or curl at the end where they are soon stranded. The netters collect their haul as soon as the tide clears the net before the gulls get to work. Several dozen fish can be taken from one trap on a favourable tide.

There are at least two ways of catching flounders with a rod. One is the crawling leger and the other is the baited spoon. A crawling leger means exactly what the name suggests. The bait is inched over the muddy sand, the movement and the displaced sand bringing the flounders in to investigate. When fishing from a boat on the drift you can obtain a similar effect by trailing the lead on the bottom. A boat normally drifts much too fast to work this trick and you have to slow it up by using either a killick or a sea anchor. I prefer a free-sliding lead of 2–3 ounces for this game with as wide a variety of bait as possible. You could start off, for instance, with small rag draped with a bit of mussel and move on to small lug, cockle or whatever is available if results are not forthcoming. From more open beaches some of my best catches of decent flounder fell to large pieces of razorfish.

In the south-east flounders start their return from deeper water in early spring. In the Stour estuary in Kent, for example, good catches start to build up around March. Flowing three-hook leger traces are widely used with small (No. 4) hooks on 6–8 lb. snoods. Weed is often a problem at this and other estuary locations. Lug is a popular bait on the Stour. Many locals believe that neap tides are the best for flounders and that the best time to start fishing is about an hour after low water, just as the tide starts to lift. On the Stour, as with many other estuaries, there is always the chance of an additional bonus in the form of a spring codling or even a few school bass.

It was John P. Garrad who drew the attention of the angling public to flounder fishing with a baited spoon (in his book *Sea Angling with a Baited Spoon*, Jenkins, 1960). After years of experiment he found that spoons about 3 inches long are best for flounders. Indeed, he states: 'As the result of thirty years' experiments I can stress that if you want flounders in numbers, nothing smaller than a 3-inch spoon will get them.' Flounders swim and feed with the current and they will not breast the current in order to chase the angler's baited spoon. The spoon must be trolled slowly *with* the current—and this means timing the speed of the boat to a nicety so that the spoon doesn't fall to the bottom and become snagged.

Baited spoons can be bought or home-made. Mine are home-made from the blades of tablespoons, the handles being cut off and a hole drilled in the narrow end to take a stainless steel split-ring to which a swivel is attached. Two further swivels joined by another split-ring are clipped into the split-ring on the spoon. A bit of strong nylon is tied to the lower swivel of the chain and to it is tied a long-shanked Size 2 hook. Some of the plastic spoons on sale are rather light although the trace carrying them can of course be leaded. John Garrad had no particular preference in bait for the baited spoon technique and reported catches on just about everything, from white and king rag to herring, sprat and mussel. The only thing he insisted on was the need to row with the flooding tide and use the estuary currents in order to get maximum results from a minimum amount of effort.

There are all sorts of variations of the baited spoon method such as trolling the spoon using an engine, deploying it on a driftline and even casting it from the shore. In the latter case the angler follows the rules by walking with the tide or by casting it into the tidal current and recovering it with the current. Nowadays, baited spoons and their variations are widely used for fish as diverse as cod and turbot.

We still don't know why flounders are attracted to spoons of a particular size although no doubt, controlled experiments in a marine aquarium would supply the answer. However, there is no doubt that a moving bait and a bait that is adorned with a spoon has a particular attraction for flatfish. I have several times seen flounders rise from the bed of a river to investigate the spoon when I have been spinning for salmon. One idea I found useful was to collect ½-inch diameter jingle bells at Christmas and to replace the flimsy wire loop at the neck with brass wire held in position with plastic body-filler. These brilliant gadgets can be strung up the trace both when fishing a spoon or when creeping a legered bait over the mud.

Not everyone is blessed with hordes of flounders in the nearest tidal channel, however, in spite of the fact that a 3-inch flounder managed to penetrate to North Woolwich, one of London's most polluted areas, and almost 25 miles from the estuary proper. This was in 1973. The north-west has been suffering a decline in flounders for some years with catches from the Mersey to the Solway Firth the lowest within living memory. In a match at New Brighton, for instance, 400 anglers only caught five flounders between them and similar reports came from Fleetwood and Blackpool. A dry spring and summer with increased abstraction and pollution are suggested as the cause although other anxious fishermen think that too much digging-out of the bait beds may be the reason. The fact remains that, at the time of writing, the flounder is diminishing in areas where it has been abundant since time out of mind.

Plaice

Many anglers are more interested in plaice than in flounders and this is so with the writer. They are a bigger, better-flavoured and more difficult fish. Although not unlike the flounder in appearance they have a smaller head and conspicuous red spots; moreover they are a lot more active than flounders. You will not find plaice on mud-flats in shallow water—they like at least a couple of fathoms of water and a good current to boot. Unlike flounders, they are predators with a particular taste for crustaceans and sand-eels.

Plaice enter most deep estuaries but, unlike flounders, they stick to the channels and are never found far from the open sea. Kennedy feels that fish are 'relatively unimportant as food for plaice' but I feel sure that this is mistaken because an excellent bait for a good plaice is a strip of mackerel. A sand-eel strip is even better. Butterfish are also reputed to be deadly as a bait for the spotted flats.

To get the biggest and best plaice you need to go offshore to where sand-eels and prawns are prolific and the tidal currents run fast. Yet with great regularity really big plaice do turn up at inshore locations such as the bars at the mouths of estuaries where they feed on material washed out of the beach by the under-tow. On some estuaries rocks will be found on either side of the mouth often with sandy mud separating low headlands from each other. These areas are raided by the local plaice on tide after tide because the reefs stretching out tend to act as 'dustbins' in which a rich marine fauna collects. Like all the smaller flats, plaice seem to prefer calm seas and neap tides for offshore feeding but when fishing from the beach I definitely like a bit of surf.

I have heard anglers condemn flatfish as uninspiring fish to catch in the sporting sense. It is true that plaice don't run like bass or bore after the manner of mullet. On the other hand they do bite vigorously and are capable of rod-bending dives mixed with plenty of 'kiting' by presenting their broad sides to the current. Consistent catches of decent-sized plaice argue that the angler not only knows his marks but knows how to fish them.

The trouble with plaice these days it that every jack-of-all trades who owns a small trawl is out hunting them. The only thing the angler can do is to get out the charts and do some figuring. Plaice like reasonably deep (3–10 fathoms) water with a tidal flow over a bottom of shell and sand, gravel or small shingle. They avoid mud and clay. So what one looks for are locations of the above general type that are hemmed in by rocks or have a scatter of rocks over the floor. There is nothing like a nice snaggy rock to discourage trawlermen! Failing this you can take your chance in the main channel in the hope that fish are coming in on the tide and they will see your bait before a trawl gets them.

I like a two-hook flowing trace for plaice when boat fishing. The sliding lead is clipped on to a Clements Boom which runs free on the main line. The flowing trace—a sensible 4 feet in length—is tied to a swivel which is in turn tied to the main line below the Clements Boom. Remembering the habits of flounders we will also need to incorporate some attractors in the basic rig. One can, of course, use the traditional coloured beads. Personally, I prefer to use the blades from a couple of leaf-shaped spoons about 1–1½ inches long. These are modified by drilling a small hole at their lower end to supplement the existing hole at their upper end. These spoon-blades are incorporated into the trace by cutting the monofil about 6 inches above each hook. The line is then tied to the top of the blade and the hook-link to the bottom. The blade thus becomes an integral part of the trace—a flashing oval of bright metal which attracts plaice for some distance.

As I said earlier, plaice are carnivores. Small sand-eels, alive or dead, should be mounted on the plaice-rig by passing the hook through a gill and nicking the point into the belly as in bass fishing. Failing sand-eels it is usually possible to obtain a few blennies about 2 inches long under stones on the shore and these are equally acceptable. As regards worm bait—I like ragworm for plaice. But don't skimp the bait by threading a single tiny rag on a small hook and expect it to catch a large plaice. Use two or three worms and let one of them hang its tail attractively.

Baited spoon will also catch plaice. Garrad records many

such catches when flounder fishing. He also reports that plaice can be caught by casting baited spoons and trolling them in the direction of the current by walking along the shore. The usual 3–3½-inch spoons seem to be best for this work.

Plaice of 2–3 lb. are not uncommon on grounds protected by natural features from the depredations of the inshore trawlers. Fish of 4–6 lb. are specimens in anyone's book and the best chance of hitting one of these in an estuary is to fish the bar at the mouth with sand-eel or prawn bait in high summer when specimens of this size do sometimes work their way inshore.

As regards shore fishing, I have done best with plaice in locations where the tidal current sweeps along the beach over a bottom of sand or shingle. Make a long, rather oblique cast and use a rolling leger. Plaice in deeper water will often move in to investigate when they spot the twinkle of the spinner-blade and will follow the bait as it rolls round and take it in quite shallow water.

The boat fishermen needs to work out a routine. Fishing on the drift seems to me the most attractive technique but a killick or sea anchor will be needed to slow the boat. A two-hook flowing trace and a bait of sand-eel or mackerel-strip is used as already described. It is sometimes an effective ploy to reel the lead well clear of the bottom and work the rod to activate the spoon-blade attractors. There is usually no need to strike because taking plaice are pretty determined fish and usually swallow the bait at the first attempt. They shouldn't be played too hard because their lively struggles coupled with the 'kiting' action brought about by their shape can easily tear the hook from a light hold.

I have much affection for plaice. They are probably the most attractive of our flatfish in appearance and from the culinary point of view are classed as a prime fish. They still remain moderately plentiful around our coasts but tax the know-how of anglers to find them in the face of commercial and semi-commercial opposition. They represent a fishing problem you can get your teeth into. There are certainly lots of local problems to solve before a box of the big spotted flats is your regular haul.

Dabs

Plaice and dabs are found on the same ground very often. However dabs are a much smaller flat than either plaice or flounders and a 2-lb. dab is a specimen. They eat a lot of baby shellfish and tube-worms as well as the usual razorfish, lug, ragworm and so on. In general habits they much resemble plaice, being fond of flowing water rather than back waters. Also they have a fondness for fish-strip and often seem to prefer it to worm.

When fishing for dabs I generally use a scaled-down version of a plaice-rig. If dabs are present on a ground I simply swop the hooks for a smaller size and make the baits more compact to suit the dab's smaller mouth. The fishing technique is the same for the two species. In fact it is no uncommon thing to catch plaice and dabs alternately during the same outing.

Opinions differ about the best state of the tide for catching dabs. I am sure that this varies between estuaries and only experiment will decide which is the best in one's own particular region. Some fishermen think that low water is best. My own experience suggests that the first of the flood up to the middle of the ebb to be best time. Certainly in one small estuary I fished you could never get dabs, or only rarely, except when the tide had started to run out. It struck me, however, that the fish probably ran in and out of the estuary on two quite different lines of travel and if one fished in both locations in succession you would probably catch dabs both coming in and going out. Garrad has a good deal to say on this subject of migration paths and it may apply to dabs as well as to flounders.

Dabs, in my view, are the most toothsome of the flats. They are rather better than plaice, being not quite so watery. They are obliging little fish and many an outing has been saved from failure by the presence of dabs on the ground. As for the various related species—witches and so forth—these are unlikely to be taken by the estuary fisher except as rare fish straying out of deep water after storms.

Turbot

Turbot or 'those tasty dustbin lids' as someone called them present a real challenge to the angler. They have a very localised distribution. As a general rule they seem to favour water between about 3 and 12 fathoms over banks of packed sand, sandy mud or shell-grit. Such banks very often lie off the mouths of estuaries. On these banks turbot have the habit of lying on the slope opposite the approaching tide-stream. This means that the bank protects them from the full force of the current and, at the same time, allows them to look upwards at what is passing overhead. When the tide changes they do the same thing in reverse, shifting to the opposite side of the bank.

Turbot are the biggest of our native flatfish—leaving aside the rare halibut—and they are wholly fish-eaters. They eat sprats, small flats, herrings, small whiting and pouting, dabs and immature flounders. However their staple diet is launce (or sand-eels), and it is no coincidence that the marine sandbanks they inhabit are locations that teem with the slender little fish. Peering up from their sandy ambush the turbot spot the launce as they pass across the bank moving with the tide. The launce realises too late that the sudden gloom is caused by the sharp-toothed mouth of a big flatfish closing around it.

Almost certainly turbot of 40 lb. exist around our coasts so the turbot of 7 to 17 lb.—which is the general run—are really no more than average for the species. Turbot is highly regarded as a fish for the table—deservedly so, I would say, because its diet is as organically pure as anything in the sea. Most anglers like to whiten the flesh by making a small slit above the tail to release the blood.

Turbot start to show up at the seaward end of estuaries from mid-July onwards. Some of them will linger around the bar feeding on the sand-eels and some may cross the bar and come a little distance up the estuary to gorge on sand-eels in the lower reaches. This activity continues until late September. No doubt turbot are also attracted by the dense shoals of 'Joeys' or harvest mackerel which swarm in the warm sea at this period during a good summer.

Most turbot-fishers think that spring tides are best for turbot and some say it is a waste of time to fish on the neaps.

As usual, there are two ways of fishing turbot from a boat—drifting and at anchor. Drifting is best if you are uncertain of the whereabouts of the big flats. However if you have cross-bearings on a likely sand-bank then it is best to anchor and shift position from time to time by streaming out more cable if the results seem slow. A few yards change in position can make a vast difference in results when turbot fishing.

A rig for turbot, as with all rigs, should be fairly spartan. The weight is on a sliding boom running up and down the main line and is retained by a swivel. The trace below is attached to the swivel with a snap-link. This trace should be as strong as the main line. It is unwise to go much below 30 lb. monofil because a big turbot levering against the pull of a spring tide needs a hefty strain to get it to the boat. A flowing two hook trace about 10 feet long is about right and it should have a swivel halfway along its length. Above the swivel many experienced turbot fishers like to place a big spoon to act as a general attractor. A spoon some 3 or 4 inches long is not too big and it can be either home-made from chromed brass or be an ordinary narrow Norwegian spoon with the treble and lower split-ring removed. The big flats don't, of course, strike at the spoon. It merely draws their attention to the baited hooks below. Hooks of from 3/0 to 6/0 are commonly used for turbot, the bait being either strips of fresh mackerel or a whole launce.

The shore fisher mustn't assume that turbot are a proposition only for the man who can plough a mile offshore in a boat. Locals at a point on the Cardiganshire coast assured me that small turbot of between 3–8 lb. often came in to feed in the mouth of a small river in late August and September and were keenly sought by fishers in the know. At the mouths of some West Country estuaries anglers fishing for bass have on occasion trodden on turbot while wading along the bar at low water, again in late summer. So the opportunity is there once the fisherman has located a suitable venue and laid his plans. For such fishing I prefer to leger with either mackerel strip or sand-eel dead-bait. If turbot refuse these then they will take nothing.

Brill

Brill are in somewhat like case. Indeed, brill and turbot often share the same ground and in the shallow estuary pools it is common to see baby brill and baby turbot, so to speak, sharing the same nursery. Brill, however, are a more active fish than turbot and they come the nearest to what could be called a sporting flatfish. A hooked brill will dive and bore with far more energy than a turbot.

The feeding activities of brill seem, so far as one can judge, to be identical to turbot. In other words it feeds on small fish with a particular preference for sand-eels. Almost oval in shape and distinctively marked brill, however, are not as large as turbot and a 10-lb. specimen is a good one.

Brill are seldom fished for specifically and the ones that are taken are usually caught in the course of turbot fishing. The same tackle and baits apply as for turbot. Good brill are sometimes caught in water no deeper than 6 fathoms when, on neap tides, they lie right on top of the sand-banks. Only rarely are they caught from the shore.

The deep narrow estuaries of the west are always worth investigating late in the summer when the possibility of big flats is raised. It is worth checking on the sand-eel population by running an eel-drag* through the loose sand at the edge of the low water-line. If plenty of eels are present they will provide bait for a fishing attempt later in the tide.

Sole

Sole are the flatfish of the epicure due to the gamey flavour they develop after being kept a day or two in the larder. They are a warm-water fish and are commonest in Britain in the south and west. Soles haunt the estuaries they favour where they consume quantities of tube-worms, small molluscs and ragworm. These fish are often overlooked by anglers due to their nocturnal feeding habits and because they tend to lurk in depressions in the seabed. A 3-lb. sole can be considered a specimen.

During the summer sole sometimes enter the bigger creeks at the seaward end of estuaries to feed on the rag swarming on

* An eel-drag or eel-rake is a curved metal implement for drawing sand-eels out of loose sand.

the mud-banks. They tolerate brackish water but seldom penetrate very far up the estuary. In spite of these estuary visits they tend to be a deep-water fish and it is my impression that they stick to the centre channel and bury themselves in the sandy mud when the ebb sets in, emerging for their feeding forays only after dark. However sole will sometimes feed in discoloured water following a storm when the water has been heavily stirred up so it would seem that the night-feeding habit is a protective instinct and a discoloured sea serves much the same purpose.

Soles like patches of sandy mud flanked by rock or adjacent to rocky ledges. With the onset of darkness they flap out of the holes where they have lain buried and begin searching for food. They appear to locate this food partly by smell and partly by investigating it with certain small organs on the underside of the head. Kennedy reports that they are fond of echinoderms—that is sand-stars and brittle stars. Quite the best bait for sole however is a plump, lively ragworm.

Sole are remarkable among our flatfishes in having a grotesquely distorted mouth. Presumably nature knows her job best and the delicious fish have no trouble in getting food between their crooked jaws. Even so, I try not to make it harder for them by using a too-large hook. Use a needle-sharp freshwater hook, say about Size 6, when fishing for sole and discard the hooks after one session. Results can be expected from dusk onwards. A two-hook leger lying flat on the bottom is the best rig for these retiring fish and you will need plenty of patience to wait while they explore your offering with their 'feelers' before they start to nibble at it.

No one is going to point out to you a location where soles lie thick in an estuary. But by shopping around and comparing the remarks made by boatmen, cockle gatherers, flounder fishers and the like and studying the large-scale map it is possible to decide on a couple of likely areas. The fact is that not many anglers have the patience to fish for sole. If you have that sort of patience then you are entitled to the culinary rewards awaiting.

Lemon sole or Lemon dab

The only other flatfish of interest to the estuary fisher is the Lemon sole or Lemon dab. Although a member of the plaice family it has an oval profile similar to the sole hence the confusion in names. Lemon dabs are not all that common in estuaries, otherwise the trawler-boys are after them very quickly. Their food is mainly baby shellfish, crustaceans and small marine worms. Lemon dabs are active little fish with a definite taste for thin strips of fish like their relatives, the plaice. A Lemon dab about a foot long is a good fish and will do his share of tugging before you get him in the boat. They are perhaps the tastiest of all the flats, soles excepted.

As with common dabs I use a scaled-down plaice-rig for the useful little fish. A two-hook flowing trace incorporating small attractors with a bait of either thinly-cut mackerel-strip or a ragworm is probably the best bet. If your boat is anchored then by all means sling in a bit of ground-bait to keep the little flats interested in your area.

Hitting on a productive location is half the problem with Lemon dabs. I know of only one really productive spot. It is a sandy bay at the mouth of a mile-wide estuary and is hemmed-in by low rocky cliffs. Several reefs extend underwater over a bottom of sand and grit and these obstacles prevent all trawling—even by the bucket-on-a-string brigade. The dabs come in on the tide and like the sheltered water which is some 2–3 fathoms deep. They seem to come in best on slackish tides when conditions are calm.

In general, fishing for flatfish in estuaries is, or can be, a productive and satisfying sport. It is also of great practical value as any housewife will tell you who is in touch with the escalating price of fish. Some of my best catches of flats have been made in estuaries and every British species can be caught therein apart from such purely deep-water species as the Megrim. Whether the giant halibut can be considered an estuary species or not I don't know, never having fished for them. Certainly halibut have been caught in deep inlets but whether these could be called estuaries is arguable.

Cod and Whiting

The movement and migration of cod

In the southern part of Britain the cod tends to be a winter visitor moving in during the autumn and moving out again in the spring. They are a cold-water fish which seem very sensitive to temperature variations. In the West Country and in West Wales, where the North Atlantic Drift tends to keep the sea temperature high, they are uncommon inshore even in winter with certain exceptions. The temperature of the sea and the movement of food species probably does much to control the migration of cod. However there is more to it than that as recent scientific work at Lowestoft and elsewhere suggests.

Cod, like most other fish, appear to flourish in cycles. There are good breeding years and poor ones and these obviously affect cod-stocks very much in terms of angling returns. An estimated 30% of cod around Britain are caught commercially each season and about 12% die naturally. The temperature of the sea appears to have a bearing on how well or how badly cod reproduce and survive, cold winters being more favourable than mild ones. The fish spawn between January and June around Britain but chiefly during the period March–April. This however is only a rough outline since there are various races of cod around our coasts and some of them, paradoxically, occur in the south-west and west. These latter fish stay in deep water offshore during the summer and only turn up in estuaries during winter and even then not in great numbers.

The inshore migration of cod centres around the migration of shoals of herring, sprats and other small fishes that are active inshore during the cold months. In the Irish Sea Kennedy reports that an analysis of 80 cod contained food as follows: Norway lobster, shrimps, sea-mice and whelks. These species, in this order, were found in 71, 15, 20 and 10 cod out of the original 80. The fact is, however, that cod will eat almost anything that comes their way provided they can swallow it down—and sometimes even if they can't. I well remember a cod I had of some 20 lb. which had a small bass stuck in its mouth with the spines of the fish running into the roof of the mouth. Grit and small stones are often found in the stomachs of cod together with sticks, plastic cups from ships and unlikely objects of all sorts. Some of these items may have been swallowed because they were encrusted with food such as Goose Barnacles.

There are two main methods of catching cod in estuaries —either by legering from the shore or from a boat or by using a big pirk or feathers from a boat or pier-head. The last method, because it has recently caught on as a novelty, will be discussed first.

Methods: pirk or feathers

Cod have been taken on feathered lures for generations which is natural enough because they are fish-eaters and the lures simulate small edible forms. Most of the cod thus caught were smallish—codling—because the feathers usually were being deployed in fairly deep water in summer by anglers in search of pollack, coalfish and mackerel. As soon as winter closed in most anglers put their feathers away and did their serious cod fishing with a traditional leger outfit. In the Firth of Clyde, however, anglers discovered that big catches of large cod could be made using home-made pirks at a mark near Dunoon known as The Gantocks. The mark is formed partly by the rough underwater ground and partly by the wreck of a Swedish ore ship. Probably other factors are involved in making this such a good mark, one of which could be the presence of vast numbers of small coalfish which seem to attract the cod in unusual numbers. Strictly speaking, the Firth of Clyde is an arm of the sea rather than an estuary. Even so, The Gantocks illustrates what occurs on a more modest scale in estuaries proper. There are many such estuaries in Scotland and further south where winter pirking will pay off provided the angler can locate a deep-water mark sheltered enough to fish by boat. Without something to attract and hold the cod on a particular location they simply stream in and out with the tide devouring what they find as they go in a random fashion.

Pirking for cod over a known mark in winter is not without finesse. It pays to cast the pirk away from the anchored boat, let it sink to the sea-bed, and work it back with small jiggling movements. Jerking or snatching should be avoided. Obviously, much depends on the type of mark. If you are fishing immediately over a wreck or over very rough ground one has no option but to try and work the pirk deep without actually fouling the structure and risking loss of tackle. In this case the use of a big single hook, possibly with a weed-guard, is a good deal safer than using a treble hook and reduces the risk of fouling considerably. If the ground is reasonably flat however then the use of a treble on the pirk may be an acceptable risk and the pirk should be sunk right to the bottom and worked back to the boat. In winter the visibility below several fathoms of water will be poor and the cod will be ranging over the mark harrying the small coalies, herring or whatever it is that attracts them. The pirk, jiggling its way over the bottom, gives them plenty of time to notice it. Experiment suggests that pirk-fishing over the ground in this manner accounts for a lot more fish than does the usual dip-and-draw technique. However, to use the method without risk to other anglers in the boat is another matter. Casting a pirk from a charter boat containing perhaps a dozen other anglers is not recommended. In any case a leaded pirk should never be swung inboard at the start of a cast or someone will get maimed. However, a couple of anglers fishing together from the stern of a boat can use the technique with profit and in safety.

There are relatively few known places where mature cod come inshore to feed regularly—places which produce very large fish like the present record 46-pounder taken from the Firth of Clyde. One such location is the Severn estuary, the north side of which has some rough ground well-known as the haunt of big cod. Indeed this area held the British record for a time before it was eclipsed by Firth of Clyde specimens. However not all anglers are interested in ultra-large cod, especially those who fish mostly for the pot. Codling of between 3–6 lb. are a far better proposition for the cook than are the coarse-flaked leviathans. Most of these codling are caught from the open shore. Sea fishing in winter from a boat off the coast is both uncomfortable and hazardous except on very favourable days. Anglers therefore take advantage of the codling's habit of feeding against a beach, especially after dark. In estuaries, on the other hand, winter boating is entirely possible and a boat enables anglers to anchor in the deeper channels where the codling are likely to run.

Codling

Cod and codling are not very active fish when hooked. They tend to bore around, offering resistance mostly by opening their huge mouths. However I noticed when taking codling from relatively shallow water such as in the Solway Firth and in the Stour estuary at Felixstowe that these fish put up a better fight than those taken from deeper water. They are of course excellent food and Kennedy rates them next to haddock. Myself, I think a well-flavoured codling, properly cooked, is as tasty as anything in British waters, salt or fresh.

Fishing for codling is a traditional sport in many estuaries. The best rig is probably a simple paternoster carrying a 3/0 or 4/0 hook. Some anglers use two hooks on double snoods but this presents problems with wind resistance when casting, the baits for codling being fairly massive. Codling are such gross feeders that it is hardly possible to over-do the portion you offer them. Bulky baits such as squid are a favourite as well as large chunks of herring or frozen mackerel. Lug is also a good codling-catcher and thousands of fish are taken annually with this bait. Although large black lug are much sought-after as a codling-bait I myself prefer the softer red type even though they need renewing on the hook fairly often. Mussel is a traditional cod bait. For shore-casting it needs to be mounted as a 'cocktail', the tougher retaining bait—squid, for example—being placed on the hook last.

Boat fishing for codling in estuaries means first of all locating a good mark. Without a mark you may well catch a couple of fish or even several fish—but the bulk of the sport will be missed as the codling stream past on the tide. Rough ground that will hold the fish and keep them foraging around is the thing to look for. If the estuary dries out such places can be found at low water. In the case of big estuaries which don't dry out one can only study the charts, watch where local boats fish and conduct trial-and-error drifts. Drifting with a pirk mounted with a single hook is one way of discovering codling marks.

In the south-west and west there is a local race of codling which spend the summer offshore in deep water and turn up in estuaries during the winter when the herring arrive. These fish are reddish in the summer—perhaps because they lurk in beds of red seaweed—but they darken on coming inshore and there is then not much to distinguish them from ordinary North Sea codling. These fish are small—from 2 to 6 lb.—and they seem to be a different type to the cod of the Severn estuary. They are variable fish and some years they fail to arrive at all. However this is true of all cod, relatively speaking. The inshore migrations, even in the prolific North Sea, are either a bumper harvest or fail to live up to expectations. We still have a lot to learn even about the humble codfish!

Haddock

The haddock shows how even a teeming species can be decimated by trawling. It is closely related to the cod and its habits are such that it used to be one of the most important demersal fishes around Britain making up half the total catch of trawlers and long-liners. However it tends to be localised in distribution with a liking for easily trawled soft ground and, unfortunately, is less prolific in its breeding than the cod. The result is that in 50 years of power-trawling around Britain the haddock has become a rare fish in the south and is far from plentiful in the north. Countless hordes of haddock used to graze the plains of ooze around our coasts and they had no answer to the scourge of mechanical inshore netting. Some day we may have the sense to stud our shallow coastal waters with obstacles to prevent inshore trawling and the haddock may come back. They are still around, especially on marks off Fowey. As a food-fish it surpasses even the cod which is reason enough to coax it back.

Whiting

If there is anywhere in Britain not visited by winter whiting I haven't heard of it. Many sea-anglers in winter rely on whiting for the bulk of their sport and are rarely disappointed. The fish have suddenly become very popular. Whiting fishing, which used to be regarded mainly as a diversion for the dark nights has become a useful way of supplementing the family deep-freezer stock. As long as this remains the case its popularity, as with cod fishing, is likely to grow.

Small herrings, tiny whiting, shrimps of various sorts and ragworms seem to form most of the diet of whiting. The fact is that whiting have distinct teeth as anyone who has inserted an incautious finger into the mouth of one can testify. Moreover they have a marked trait towards cannibalism and one of the best baits for whiting is a strip from a whiting. This applies even to quite small fish. As an experiment I once tried lowering tiny strips of whiting-skin to a shoal of whiting no bigger than about 3 inches long and they seized the bait with relish. They are predators as distinct from the omnivorous cod and the crustacean-eating haddock. Even so, whiting do like lugworm especially the red variety and some of my best catches were taken on this bait. When boat fishing in deep water for big whiting coming straight in from the open sea I found that mussel had an attraction for the fish which exceeded their interest in either worm or mackerel-strip.

Whiting are pretty erratic fish and whenever I have heard a fisherman say: 'They come in with the first frosts' I have heard another say: 'They like mild weather.' Moreover the time of their coming can't be predicted. I have caught whiting that have come inshore in late September when mackerel were still in the water. During another season, however, they have not turned up till late November or December. Sometimes the shoals are of relatively big fish—and a 2-lb. whiting is a good one—whereas, some winters, the run consists of fish no bigger than $\frac{3}{4}$ lb. Even more curious, the shoals of decent fish are often restricted to one area while other areas are plagued with the small stuff.

Why this should be so is a puzzle. It seems to have nothing to do with the herring-movements or even with the weather because whiting will take in a flat calm or in a storm—if they're around, that is. Why they come and where they go seems to baffle old anglers as well as newcomers. All you can do is to fish and if whiting are there you'll know about it soon enough.

Whiting give a characteristic and vigorous bite that makes the rod-bell tinkle. However I don't care much for rod-bells and prefer to keep a tight line and await the jag-jag pull of the taking fish. Sometimes, however, the lead will slide slyly towards you, resulting in a sudden decrease in tension, as a good whiting swims up and towards you with the bait. On giving an instant strike you will nearly always have him.

Sometimes cod and whiting are found together on the same mark although this is not usual. The two species generally keep apart, possibly because large cod eat the smaller fish. Many anglers welcome the cod-grounds being occasionally invaded by whiting because the latter give much faster sport. Even so, they can be fairly selective in their feeding. They like fresh rather than preserved bait and seem to have different preferences on different grounds. Red lug, hooked so that the juices are retained, has been a fine bait on most of the locations I've fished with mussel a close second. However—as mentioned earlier—sometimes the situation is reversed and lug is a second-best bait to mussel. Whiting will also take herring and mackerel-strip but neither are as good as lug or mussel in my experience.

A lot depends on when and where you are fishing. In deep estuaries whiting take freely even in daytime provided the water is over about 6 fathoms deep in the channel. They only enter shallow water when the light is spent and even then they seem to avoid backwaters and stick to where there is a tidal flow. It seems probable that they come in after certain food-species. Observation suggests that the commonest of these is small pouting which often teem in the inshore sea during the winter.

Paternoster is the rig most whiting fishers use with slight variations suggested by local experience. Two or three hooks on fairly short snoods about a foot apart are sufficient. Stainless steel hooks are much better than so-called 'whiting' hooks which are generally coarse in the barb and thick in the wire.

Whiting can be caught in the surf on the open beach and these fish are often big ones running between $1\frac{1}{2}$ and $2\frac{1}{2}$ lb. My impression is that they come in like bass to feed in the undertow as individuals. Further up an estuary whiting can be caught from the shore or from a boat. Shore fishing is best after dark whereas boat fishing over a good deep mark can be successful during the day. As with cod, whiting seem to be stimulated to come inshore following a gale especially if this coincides with a spring tide. However, unlike cod, whiting are not really a cold-water fish and this fact undoubtedly explains their presence in quantity in the south-west and west where the bulk of cod do not penetrate.

I have known anglers to launch their dinghies even in winter and put out a few hundred yards into the open sea in search of whiting. It can be done safely but only if you watch the weather constantly and follow the rules rigorously. However, even the sheltered waters of estuaries can be hazardous in the winter. The main danger, in my experience, is the shortness of the day. By fishing awkward tides you are often tempted to linger on a mark longer than you should and eventually have to land in near-darkness. After a few hair-raising experiences of this sort I fish only winter tides which enable the boat to get back in daylight even if this means cutting the fishing short.

Somehow whiting have always seemed to me a fish that is characteristic of the winter scene, like herring. Whiting fishing can become almost a ritual. On our part of the coast most whiting fishers know each other by name having met each other at one time or another on dark beaches under Tilley lamps or in the yellow gleam of jetty lights. Muffled in oilskins and braced against the icy wind, the whiting fisher is a distinctive phenomenon on the angling scene in which like soon recognises like. In the winter darkness the estuary takes on a vastly different appearance than in the balmy days of summer. The unexpected lights of farmsteads shine through the gloom on the hillsides and reflect briefly in the chill water. The spectacle of gleaming whiting coming up kicking in the lamplight never fails to bring the fisher back winter after winter to try his luck and exchange fishing gossip.

The best of estuary whiting fishing, however, is on a crisp autumn morning when we have loaded our tackle into the boat and are gliding down-river to meet the first of the tide. Amidships is half a bucket of fat mussels and some plump lug. The mark is only half a mile away—it is a location found by chance a few yards inside the navigation buoy marking the main channel. It seems to be a patch of rough ground with a profuse growth of red seaweed on it which no doubt harbours hordes of small pouting, poor cod and similar baitfish. The water here is deepish being about 9 fathoms even at low water.

After bringing the boat on to the mark we drop anchor. We have never had an anchor caught up on this mark so far but take the precaution of 'tripping' it. In other words, the anchor rope is shackled to the anchor crown and then led along the shank to which it is secured by a single turn of cord. We know from experiment that a sudden tug on the rope will snap this cord and let us draw the anchor up by the crown should the flukes become jammed on a rock.

Our ground-bait canister is lowered at the bow and jiggled around as it goes down. It contains a slushy mess of offal, broken crabs and several very ripe herrings, well broken up. This mixture will soon attract a lot of small pout, we hope, which will in turn—again we hope—attract something better. While the ground-bait is doing its work we have a look at our tackle.

It is going to be a neap tide so the tidal speed will not be too fast. We reckon we can fish this mark using leads starting at 3 ounces and going up to 6 ounces without losing bottom. We take our time baiting the two hooks on the paternoster rig. We put a mussel on one and secure it with a 'tip' of toughish squid tentacle and put a couple of small red lug on the other. We again give the bait canister a shake and, now the tide has definitely started to flood, lower the baited hooks over the stern and let the multiplier run the lead to the sea floor.

Almost at once we feel small pout starting to pick at the baits. This is what usually happens before the whiting arrive and it means the ground-bait is working. We give the canister a further shake for luck and at the same moment get a dragging bite that is certainly no pouting. Nor is it. It's a dogfish! We rebait and wait a few minutes before lowering the lead again. The tide is now flowing well and after only a few moments' wait our rod raps with the urgent signal that the first whiting has arrived. We swing it aboard to find it is a nice fish of just over 1½ lb.

Sport along these lines continues with breaks—a long one occurring at the top of the tide—until the darkening afternoon suggets the time has come to pack up. By now we have about three dozen whiting in the box together with a few dabs and one small plaice. The whole outing has been fairly typical even to the chill wind which has now sprung up and which flicks the odd bit of spray into our faces from the bow at the boat heads for shore.

Not all estuaries run quantities of winter cod and whiting but even those, such as the Mersey, which used to be grossly polluted have their quota which diligent fishers can discover if they search around. Codling of 5½ lb. have been taken recently off Wallasey which used to be one of the most polluted parts of the Mersey estuary. Lines set further out have collected cod up to 9 lb. and whiting up to 2 lb. One can only deduce that attempts to clean up what used to be one of the most badly polluted estuaries in the world have started to pay off. The same could also be said of the Thames estuary where some good catches of codling are taken regularly.

Pouting

Most deepish estuaries contain pouting, especially small ones. However if there are plenty of rocky clefts in the floor of the estuary with a good depth of water the pouting may weigh up to a couple of pounds. High up Milford Haven there is an underwater 'canyon' giving a depth of over 14 fathoms even at low water. In November it is full of pouting because these fish, above anything, are lovers of rocky ground.

The pouting is a deep-bodied fish, reddish-brown in colour, with a distinctive solitary barbel under its chin. It seems to regard estuaries as nursery areas and, as it reaches maturity, it moves out to rocks, reefs and rough ground offshore where the feeding is better. Big pouting are often found in the vicinity of wrecks.

Pouting are a much less vigorous fish than whiting. Their teeth are smaller than those of whiting and they show no tendency to shoal and hunt their prey over long distances as whiting do. If you want a big pouting in an estuary—and they reach over 5 lb.—you need to locate a wreck. Although they will take mackerel-strip and small pirks they seem to prefer worm and crustacean baits. Pouting have little sporting value but they do make quite a tasty meal even though the flesh is a bit watery.

Coalfish

Estuary fishers in winter may well encounter coalfish since this species tend to migrate inshore with the onset of cold weather. In fact small coalfish (two-year-olds) are something of a pest on many marks since they grab bait intended for better fish. These young coalies are usually no more than about 7 or 8 inches long and it is often their presence in numbers which attracts the winter cod. Quite possibly they move inshore in an instinctive attempt to avoid the cod.

I would not rate coalfish as an important estuary fish, however, at least not from the angling point of view. Big coalfish like deep water well offshore although big fish sometimes move inshore during rough winter weather, probably chasing the herring. The small coalfish—commonly known as 'billet' —keep pretty much within the 10 fathom line.

Coalfish are sometimes mistaken for pollack although, in my opinion, they are a far more handsome fish, dark green in colour shading to black on the back with a white stripe along the lateral line which is most distinctive. Occasionally, in the west, we get shoals of small coalfish moving inshore in October and November weighing between 2–3 lb. They sometimes take baits such as mackerel-strip, razorfish or lug that were intended for a late bass. Like the pollack, however, they are not a very good table fish, the flesh being watery and flavourless.

Pollack are not really an estuary fish although it is claimed that big pollack will sometimes chase sand-eel shoals up the tidal channel during high summer. There are usually plenty of small pollack around the seaweed-covered rocks fringing the mouths of larger estuaries and numbers of these are caught by holidaymakers spinning for mackerel. Kennedy notes that pollack enter the estuaries of rivers such as the Munster Blackwater to feed on migrating smolts in the spring. Such activity may be more widespread than is suspected as I heard a similar story from Wales.

CHAPTER NINE

Small Fish and Unusual Fish

Mackerel

There is a sense in which mackerel and whiting can be considered as mirror images of each other. They are similar in size and in their habits of congregating in large shoals. But whereas the whiting is a bottom feeder which approaches the shore in winter the mackerel is a surface feeder which approaches the shore in summer. Both are predators and both are much sought-after by the angling community.

Mackerel start to enter estuaries from July onwards. In small estuaries they come in and go out on the bigger tides in pursuit of their summer fare which consists of any fry that is in great abundance but especially baby herrings, pilchards and rocklings which are collectively described as 'brit'. In bigger estuaries they remain throughout the tide, moving into channels and deeper holes at low water. In Milford Haven mackerel commonly penetrate 7 or 8 miles inland and can be seen at low water playing about like trout.

Size for size, mackerel are the most sporting of our native sea fishes if caught on suitably light gear. On a fly-rod they are probably stronger than a sea-trout of similar size. Being prolific and not hard to catch mackerel tend to be underrated by fishermen. One often notices a sort of snobbery among anglers in that mackerel are rather contemptuously hauled aboard on a string of feathers for bait while the angler then devotes enormous concentration on fishing for much less sporting and often inedible species. If mackerel were rather uncommon they would be among the most prized fish around our coasts. Alas, such is human nature.

After leaving deep water where they have spent the winter they move towards their spawning grounds south-west of Land's End. Most of the spawning seems to be in April after which the vast shoals continue moving towards the coast, breaking up into smaller shoals as they go. From June onwards the feeding begins in earnest as schools of mackerel ruthlessly hunt hordes of brit up and down the coast.

When they are feeding mackerel will seize any small object that glitters but when they are not feeding they are almost impossible to budge no matter what sort of lure is deployed. I have fished tides that produced big catches. Yet the next tide has produced nothing even though mackerel were plainly around. They seem to feed best during spells of fine weather and worst during rough and unsettled conditions when the barometer is low.

Fishing for mackerel with a light spinning rod, fixed-spool reel and 6 lb.-monofil line using a narrow Norwegian spoon about $1\frac{1}{2}$ inches long is a sporting and practical approach. Although they tend to feed near the surface most of the time this is not always the case. If you fail to get takes when spinning near the top it pays to let the spoon sink to some depth before starting recovery. Occasionally they are very deep, even on the bottom. If there is a hazard due to weed catching the spoon it is good practice to start counting the instant the lure hits the surface after casting. After a bit of trial-and-error one soon learns to estimate exactly how far to let the lure sink in order to catch fish and not weed. Like most fish, mackerel tend to refuse a spinner with weed draped on it.

Catching mackerel from a boat using light tackle can be hectic. They run at great speed, diving as they go and often end up under the keel. This is not so important with dinghies that are regularly brought ashore and are therefore clean under the hull. But with heavier boats which have picked up a barnacle or two the result is almost certainly that your line will be cut. Many a mackerel has won its liberty by running the line over a foul bottom.

Mackerel can be caught when legering using ragworm or lug as bait. This method is particularly good in the early autumn when their attention appears to switch to the lower levels of the sea. Many of these bait-caught mackerel are big fish of 2 lb. and upwards. The fact is that bait-feeding mackerel from the bottom seem to have acquired a different sort of behaviour from that of the smaller shoal fish.

The present record mackerel of 5 lb. 6 ounces should be compared to the average shoal fish which varies between $\frac{3}{4}$–$1\frac{1}{4}$ lb. Later in the summer the average weight of shoal mackerel seems to drop even further as the inshore waters are invaded by 'harvest mackerel' which are sometimes as small as ½ lb. Mackerel are rather slow-growing fish and to reach a weight of several pounds it seems obvious that such individuals are either very old or, more likely, have adopted a different diet to the generality. This trait occurs in other fish—lake trout for example. Outsized mackerel probably reach this size in a reasonable time because they have adapted to some form of bulk diet.

One of the most entertaining ways of catching mackerel is with a trout fly-fishing outfit. A good place for this is at the mouth of an estuary where there are rocks covered in kelp. You start fishing just as the tide starts to lift. I use large sea-trout flies for this sport, patterns such as Teal-and-silver and Silver Blue being quite effective. It can be quite exciting fun because there is always the risk of a pollack plunging at the fly or even a bass or a sea trout. But even if you hook nothing bigger than a 1-lb. mackerel it is by no means easy on light gear to steer it away from the kelp. Some sort of landing net is essential or it will work its way into the weed the moment you try to get it ashore.

It is a great pity that so many anglers restrict their mackerel fishing to feathering with heavy tackle merely to catch bait. Even worse, many newcomers receive their first introduction to angling after being taken out on a boat-trip in which lines fastened to heavy leads are dragged behind the boat and festooned with feathers on which mackerel are hauled aboard literally by the dozen. No fish can possibly show any sporting characteristics in such circumstances.

Mackerel need to be eaten fresh from the sea if their full flavour is to be appreciated. The flesh is extremely rich and tends to be slightly oily although much depends on what they have been eating prior to capture. Smoked and lightly cooked within an hour of being taken from the salt there is perhaps no British fish better in flavour with the possible exception of a small codling.

Herring

Another small but prolific fish the angler may encounter is the herring. Herrings, of course, are the traditional 'bread and butter' fish of the sea. For some reason herrings have a distinct liking for brackish water although what attracts them is something of a mystery. Dense shoals of herring start to come inshore during October and November when some of them find their way up estuaries. If the water is deep enough they will stay there over several tides until they are finally scattered by predators such as spurdogs.

If he is lucky the angler may see a phenomenon relating to herrings that is seldom mentioned, even by the biology books. I have only seen it once. As the herring come into shallow estuarial water they become very excited and mill around busily. The observer then notices a dark globular mass and finds that it is composed of herring packed into a sphere so the fish are touching. These spheres or 'herring balls' may be six feet in diameter and contain thousands of fish. The whole thing is in constant motion, herrings constantly wriggling out of the ball and then diving in again. I have cast a line over such a ball to see what would happen. What happens is that the ball moves away slowly almost as if it had a single intelligence guiding it. There are biological reasons why this may be so. However, why herrings act this way seems to be unknown.

Herring feed mainly on plankton, krill, amphipods and tiny organisms of various sorts. Like most sea fish they are opportunists and will also devour fish-fry and sand-eels if small enough. This makes them a fair target for the angler because, although there is no way of using plankton as a bait on a hook, it is certainly possible to simulate tiny fish and catch herrings on artificial lures.

Float-fishing for herring seems to have first developed in the south-west in various harbours and estuarial waters where the fish congregate during the winter year after year. A float and a flowing trace below a bit of lead wire seems to be the common routine. Three or four size 10 freshwater hooks are used, one tied to the foot of the trace and the others on snoods or droppers let into the main line. Bait is usually small harbour ragworm. Herring hooked a few feet below the surface using this technique put up a far better fight than do fish hooked at great depth. The quick reduction in pressure on fish drawn up from a great depth has a devastating effect on the swim-bladders of fish even to the extent of splitting their guts. I have never tried the float method but understand that scores of fish can be caught once the angler learns how to time his strikes. However, catching herring near the surface is usually night-fishing and some form of illumination is essential. Either a portable light on a pole or overhead jetty lights are necessary in order to see the float. Moreover lights at night do seem to have an attraction for many sorts of fish including herring.

While prospecting Milford Haven I discovered that herring come in and lie in shoals in the deep trenches in that waterway. During the day, at low water, they lie near the bottom. The main problem was what to attract them with in that location, the water being between 60 and 100 feet deep. Milford anglers had noticed that herring were occasionally caught on mackerel feathers in late autumn. The idea of a feathered lure designed specifically for herring evolved spontaneously among a number of anglers and resulted in a wide variety of lures in an equally wide range of colours. The lure that seemed to give the best results was tied on to a size 8 T.D.E. freshwater hook with a long shank. The part of the shank nearest the eye was dressed with tinsel. Then a piece of red or orange plastic tube was worked over the bend of the hook and whipped firmly in position. This thin tube was obtained from electric flex by splitting the tube with a razor-blade. The fact that it could thus be partly opened-out made it easier to fit on to the shank. Once the tube was in position it was clipped so that it overhung the bend of the hook by about ½ inch. This overhanging portion was then reduced in diameter with the razor-blade to give it extra flexibility.

Drifting over the herring marks in daylight I found that these odd little lures definitely worked. They were tied on to a trace, three at a time, with a space of about a foot between each lure. They were operated with a slow sink-and-draw motion and seemed to do best on the ebbing tide. The shoal seemed to be lying in a cigar-shaped formation with its narrow end pointing up-tide and the boat had to be positioned fairly exactly at the start of each drift if the rod was to take any fish. The bites registered on the lures began to cease as the water fell away towards half-tide and finally stopped altogether.

After studying various reference books on marine life I am still at a loss to know why herring take a lure of this sort. It is possible that they look rather like larval smelts although it must be admitted that the smelt is greenish-olive rather than red or orange. Maybe a lure dressed with green tubing would be more effective than the ones described. Herring fishers may care to experiment further on these lines.

Herring are not a sporting fish when taken from deep water. Even so, they are quite attractive in appearance and, of course, are one of the most nutritious fish in the sea. Lightly smoked and grilled within an hour or two of capture, the humble herring is a dish fit for an epicure which is more than can be said for the stale, long-dead fish on fishmongers' slabs which are the best most people get.

It is a curious and unexplained fact that there is a connection between the shoaling of herring and the phases of the moon. The biggest hauls of herring are usually made during the full moon period at which time the fish seem more active than usual. Herring drifters often make a point of fishing during the full moon phase knowing that this is the best time for a bumper catch. It is my belief that the moon does indeed exert an influence on animals and plants. Certain sorts of marine worms seem to be stimulated by the moon as do certain insects. It is probably the increased activity by food organisms eaten by the herring during the full moon period which causes the activity on the part of the fish.

Shad

Two sorts of shad, the Twaite and the Allis, which are also members of the herring family, are likely to be met with on larger estuaries. Southend on the Thames estuary and the estuary of the Severn are places where these fish can be encountered. Twaite shad used to be seen in the Solent and Southampton Water although recent reports from that area are few. The Allis has been reported from the Avon and the Twaite shad from the Wye estuary.

Shad take a spinner and they are usually fished for very much as if they were mackerel. Spinning for Twaite shad is quite a feature of angling in the Severn estuary in spring. The Allis shad is the larger of the two species and is said to reach a length of a couple of feet and a weight of around 8 lbs. The present record ($3\frac{1}{4}$ lbs.) is therefore well below the maximum weight possible for the species.

As regards sporting qualities, I have heard various opinions expressed. Never having fished for shad, it is impossible to comment usefully. These fish contain a mass of tiny bones like others of the herring family but are spoken of well by those who have eaten them.

Unusual captures

Here is a true story about a gigantic rarity in estuary fish, one that the angler is unlikely ever to see let alone catch. I refer to the sturgeon.

One day in early summer, before the war, an angler was spinning a pool at the head of the tide on the River Towy. Behind him he heard what he took to be a section of bank fall into the water, the upheaval was so huge. He forgot the incident until he returned the next evening to spin over the same pool, hoping to get a sea-trout. Suddenly, his small minnow became stuck in what he assumed was an underwater snag.

Pulling on the minnow from all angles produced no result and he was about to break the line when he noticed that the 'snag' was moving slowly around the pool. There was no question of playing the object since even maximum pressure had not the slightest effect on it. The angler simply paid out line and reeled it in while he tried to see what on earth was on the other end.

At that point the object decided it didn't like the pool and made a bid to go down a long shallow run leading to the tideway below. Halfway down it touched bottom and became stranded. The fisherman abandoned his rod and shouted for a friend to help. Luckily he had with him a strong, sharp gaff. Using the gaff and throwing their arms around they managed to drag it to dry shingle.

The monster was a fish big enough to boggle the imagination. It was a hen sturgeon, over 7 feet long, weighing upwards of 370 lb.

The first problem was the question of transportation. It was now getting late and the local farmer was in bed. When asked if he would harness a horse and cart to bring a fish up from the river he thought the suggestion was a leg-pull in very poor taste. Eventually, he was persuaded and the great fish was finally hauled up to a beam in the barn when several buckets of ova ran out of it which the farmer fed to his pigs. In the end the sturgeon ended up at Billingsgate after being declined by the king.

Whether the sturgeon actually took the minnow into its mouth and was thus fairly hooked is not known because during the struggle to get it ashore the lure became detached from the fish. The man who caught the huge fish—whom I know well—always insisted that there was no way of being certain.

It seems reasonable to give the benefit of the doubt and to declare that this was the biggest fish ever caught in fresh or brackish water in Britain since records began. Nor is it likely to be beaten because the odds against such a freak capture must run into millions to one against. Sturgeon must once have been common in our rivers and estuaries but pollution, netting and obstructions across rivers have almost extinguished the species in Britain. About one sturgeon on average is caught each year by trawlers. This fact alone shows the fantastic nature of the feat.

However there is a difference between freak captures and unusual captures. Among the latter must certainly be included various sub-tropical fish which reach our shores on the North Atlantic Drift every season during high summer. As a matter of fact some of these fish are not all that unusual and a few of them, such as the bonito, have already found their way into the record list while others, such as the filefish, are almost common.

Actually two sorts of bonito visit these coasts—the Oceanic Bonito and the Belted Bonito or pelamid. Being very similar it takes an expert to tell which is which, however. Nor is it too clear which species is the more common around Britain. Possibly it is the pelamid because it is this species which has got into the British list with a specimen of 8 lb. 13 ounces caught in 1969 at Torbay. I have never landed a pelamid although I believe I have hooked them. This season I saw a specimen of about 6 lb. performing the characteristic trick of the species of 'walking' on the water by flicking its tail very rapidly. It is this habit which gives pelamids the popular name of 'skipjack'.

These large, speedy members of the mackerel family are seldom seen around British coasts before July when the water becomes really warm. There is not much doubt in my mind that the thing that attracts them are the dense shoals of common mackerel. A pelamid a yard long will devour up to a dozen mackerel at a sitting.

These strong, ocean-going fish only enter the outer extremities of estuaries. They like fast tidal currents and it is on the surface of these that they can be seen skipping along on their tails almost in the manner of a flying-fish. Whether they do this for fun or to dodge a bigger predator below I don't know.

Most pelamids are caught by chance around Britain by anglers who are using lures for other species, often mackerel and pollack feathers. Probably if larger lures were used in likely areas a lot more pelamids would be caught. Observation convinces me that they are by no means uncommon along the south and west coasts during a hot summer. However, there is now a growing awareness that these fish do migrate as far as Britain and it is only a matter of time before experts at pelamid fishing develop.

Although I have never landed a pelamid I believe I have been broken a couple of times by the giant mackerel. When common mackerel shoal in order to feed on brit all the secondary predators in the area close in to feed on the mackerel. When spinning for mackerel in such conditions I have, at different times, been broken by large, fast-taking fish which made a long run quite unlike that of a bass or even a tope. The chances are that they were pelamids because it is usually in these very conditions that most specimens caught around Britain are captured.

The spin-fisherman who wants to try his hand with this junior member of the tunny family should use a 3-inch wobbling spoon around the fringes of a mackerel shoal in late July and August during a warm summer. The reel should carry about 300 yards of 10-lb. line to allow a reasonable safety margin and even then your resources may be taxed. For instance, there is reason for thinking that albacores also come up to our shores after mackerel and these are a bigger fish than pelamids, going as big as 20 lb. or more.

A sub-tropical well worth including in the British list is the Trigger fish. This year (1973) they have been almost common, even turning up for sale on fishmongers' slabs. Specimens were caught at the top end of the Towy estuary and in Milford Haven. Local newspapers printed pictures of the flat-sided, bream-like creatures until they ceased to be a novelty. Trigger fish however have not much sporting or culinary value. The most that can be said for them is that they add a touch of the exotic to the angling scene.

Another small fish often encountered in estuaries is the garfish. It is an odd creature with green bones, somewhat resembling a swordfish, although it is vaguely related to the flying-fishes. Fishing for garfish, using the lightest of spinning tackle, is very entertaining because they exhibit all the qualities of a sporting sea fish in miniature including speedy runs along the surface, jumping, and the ability to shed the hook and escape in two cases out of three.

Although they are sometimes called the 'mackerel guide' garfish work their way in from deep water much earlier than do the mackerel. I have caught them in Milford Haven in April—at least two months before the shoals of mackerel arrive. On the other hand their season inshore seems to be much shorter than mackerel and you seldom hear of a gar being caught after mid-summer.

Most garfish are caught by accident while the angler is fishing for mackerel. Often there is a sprinkling of gars among the early mackerel shoals and this is how one usually encounters them. Although Kennedy says that garfish congregate in shoals I have never seen this occur and fancy it must be a trait of the open sea rather than inshore.

Most of the gars around my part of the coast are a foot to eighteen inches long although bigger ones, up to a yard long, are said to occur. They seem to feed on fry much in the way that mackerel do; they take a spinner readily. This raises the question of their elongated snipe-like beak and what role this plays in food collecting. My own hunch is that the feeding habits of garfish vary according to the season and that for the most part, they feed on marine worms. No one, however, has so far described how garfish use their snipe-like beaks to dig worms from their burrows. Yet what other use it could have is hard to figure.

The trouble with trying to catch garfish with a spinner is that they grab the lure with their long beak and tend to miss the hook entirely. When gars are plentiful it is well worth while to use ragworm fished on a small hook below a float. They seem to take a bait of this sort far more positively into their mouths than they do with a spinner and a far higher proportion become hooked.

CHAPTER TEN

Estuary Slob and Sea Trout

Slob

Fishing for migratory trout in the brackish water of an estuary offers unexcelled sporting oportunities both for fly-fishers and those who prefer to spin. It must, of course, be the right sort of estuary. The river, in other words, must contain brown trout and sea-trout so this rules out heavily polluted streams and rivers where coarse fish predominate. Even so, there are many scores of small rivers in the south, the West Country, all along the Welsh coast and the north-west coast, and in Scotland and Ireland where fishing the estuary is a valid and interesting approach to game fishing.

An ideal estuary, to my mind, is one with a long sandy or gravelly series of beaches with sparse vegetation on the banks. It will be wide and shallow rather than narrow and deep. This fact facilitates wading. The configuration of the ideal estuary lends itself to fishing in that, at low water, there are pools connected to runs just as in the purely freshwater reaches. The ebbing tide may even expose a couple of low waterfalls. If, on top of all this, the estuary is reasonably isolated with plenty of inexpensive river fishing in the locality to mop up the anglers, you may well find you have a first-class fishing venue all to yourself.

Slob or estuarine trout are simply ordinary brown trout that have dropped down to the estuary to enjoy the improved feeding to be found there. Brown trout in most rain-fed rivers do, in fact, move about quite freely and they 'migrate' from reach to reach according to conditions. Not all of them get down as far as the estuary however. Modern exploitation of rivers with its attendant water-abstraction seems to me to be forcing brown trout ever more into a migratory situation. When rivers drop to a low level during the summer the brown trout have every incentive to move down to where the feeding is good and the water plentiful.

Estuary trout usually become lighter in colour when

they have been some time in brackish water and a few may in fact turn silvery. How long they spend in the estuary depends, I feel sure, on the prevailing level of the river, floods encouraging them to move upstream. In a wet season therefore the slob trout population of an estuary is probably at its minimum.

Very few anglers set out specifically to catch slob trout, at least not on most rivers. Certainly I don't. Most of us fish for sea-trout and if a slob trout takes the lure then so be it—it is simply a welcome addition to the catch. Since the same techniques and methods will catch both sorts of fish we will continue the chapter considering sea-trout and sea-trout only.

Sea-Trout

Sea-trout can be expected early in the season in some estuaries. It is not uncommon for salmon fishermen to catch them in February and March although they seldom appear in any quantity until late April or May. The early fish are usually big ones and are not particularly easy to catch. A proportion of them have spawned two or three times before and, quite possibly, have had previous dealings with anglers. I have the impression that they don't linger too long in the estuary but move up briskly into the river's middle reaches on some convenient flood. The opportunity for catching these fish in brackish water at the beginning of the season is therefore limited.

The best of estuary fishing is in late May, June, July and early August. The estuary is now well-stocked with feed and sea-trout have less inclination to roam the coast with so many easy meals for the taking. Sand-eels—inevitably—are high on the menu for sea-trout together with sand-shrimps, prawns and other crustaceans and the fry of many sorts of fish. In these conditions sea-trout drift up and down with the tides stuffing themselves with nourishment. Smolts which went down to the sea in the spring weighing a few ounces become fish of between $\frac{1}{2}$ lb. and $1\frac{1}{4}$ lb. within a few months. As these fish move to the top of the estuary in late summer they will provide the fisher with some of his busiest sport.

The bigger sea-trout—fish of between 2–8 lb.—come in from the open sea to feed in estuarial water but at a less furious pace than the young whitlings. Many of them are maiden fish preparing to run the river for their first breeding season. They have great deep shoulders and small heads with bodies as shining as polished steel.

The angler prospecting an estuary needs to discover just how far upstream the tidal influence extends. What happens in many cases is that the tidal influence is produced by the river backing up on itself as the downward flow is halted and reversed by the rising tide. Although this is technically the top of the estuary, the water is in fact fresh.

I have always found this point on estuaries a good place to fish. Sea-trout lying in the pools and runs seem to be greatly stimulated by the tidal effect and for perhaps half an hour prior to the arrival of the freshwater 'bulge' moving upstream they will start to rise keenly. The well-thrown fly then finds plenty of takers, especially towards dusk. This far up the estuary the tidal effect may be only a couple of feet deep. However the fish seem to detect it easily and react with vigour. Moreover, fresh fish will be moving up from the lower estuary and if a shoal of these arrives then the sport should be hectic.

Fly-fishing

Fly-fishing in brackish water does little harm to freshwater gear provided it is swilled in freshwater after use. However, I find that you do have to keep an eye on rod-rings and aluminium reel fittings. This is particularly the case when you are tempted to work your way down the estuary to the more saline regions.

As regards rods, much depends on the size of the estuary you intend to fish and its relative wadeability. It is hopeless to cover a really broad stream with an 8-foot trout rod. To fish it properly you may well have to use a light salmon rod of about 12 foot handling an AFTM 6 line. If the stream is smaller and you can wade a third of the way across then a rod of $9\frac{1}{2}$ or 10 feet with line and reel to match will certainly provide better sport with whitling and will deal also with the bigger fish.

For many years I used nothing but silk fly-line because I prefer it to synthetic lines. At the moment there is an upsurge of interest in silk lines, many newcomers having discovered that it has virtues they never suspected. There is however one snag—it needs greasing with mucilin which detergents remove. Almost every river in Britain today—except remote Highland streams—carries a summer scum of detergent. The foul and quite unnecessary chemical is omnipresent. The puzzled angler who notices that there is not even a house on the river he fishes and wonders about this detergent scum should be aware that farmers sluice their dairies down twice a day with the wretched stuff and telltale suds soon appear in the local stream. These suds wipe the mucilin from a fly-line within minutes and leave it in a sinking and waterlogged state. Reluctantly therefore I have had to start using synthetic lines of the floating/sink tip sort. The use of needless chemicals is fostered by firms who make them for profit and have not the slightest regard for the environment. Apart from sinking fly-lines detergents also destroy aquatic flies on which fish feed. Shareholders in the firms concerned should, by law, be appraised of these facts when the state of their dividends is quoted. They would then, at least, not be able to pretend ignorance.

As regards flies for estuary fishing—a fairly simple principle operates. Insect life in brackish water is negligible. Seatrout, therefore, cannot feed on insects in this environment. The flies that catch sea-trout in estuaries are really lures or simulations of marine food-forms such as shrimps and small sand-eels. At any rate they seem to be taken by the fish as representing these creatures.

For some reason I have never been able to discover the Teal, blue and silver combination is one of the most deadly colour-schemes ever invented for sea-trout whether in brackish or freshwater. If I had to be restricted to one fly over a whole season the Teal–blue–silver is the one I would choose. And not only for sea-trout. I have had lake trout up to 5 lb. in Ireland on this pattern as well as three salmon within the hour when using it on the Towy. Writers have been commenting on the virtues of the Silver-blue since the days of Hamish Stuart, over 70 years ago, to T. E. Dutton writing in 1972. My advice is to stock your fly-box quite heavily with this pattern in sizes from, say, 6–10 and styles ranging from bushy dressings you can use as a top dropper to sparse dressings that would serve as a point fly. Moreover it should be remembered that 'blue' does not specify the material. In practice one normally encounters blue-dyed cocks' hackles and these are quite effective. But blue jay is at least as effective, maybe even more so if there is any substance in the theory that it reacts to ultraviolet.

I have caught some good sea-trout on tube flies. It is certainly the case that the small treble hook tied on the leader at the tail of these flies gives the angler a better chance of landing sea-trout in brackish water than does a single hook. Fresh sea-trout—whitling especially—have relatively soft mouths and they not infrequently manage to shed the hook by jumping and tearing it from their mouths. A small treble helps mitigate this happening.

From deep dusk onwards and even in daylight if there is a good flow of water coming down-river, a two-hook lure about $2\frac{1}{2}$ inches long can be very effective. These lures can be hairwings or be dressed with feathers. Some anglers like an ordinary Black Lure for this style of fishing but I myself prefer the Teal–blue–silver combination.

Locations

It may be useful to describe actual locations on one or two different estuaries together with notes about the situation as it occurs, so to speak, on the ground. Before the River Authority tried to 'improve' the upper part of the Teifi estuary by trying to turn it into a canal there was a variety of estuary venues which nearly always produced a few fish. You started on the run below the castle which was about as far as the tide reached. When the water was low and owls hooted in the summer twilight it was always worth running a fly under the trees although the wading was very dangerous being slate slabs.

Below this run was a long, fast glide which always looked good for a fish but never produced a thing all the time that I knew it. Below this again was a wonderful run, slow, well-shaded and backed by a rock bluff soaring upwards over 300 feet. This run was a favourite lie for whitling and small sea-trout up to about 2 lb. By casting directly across and allowing the line to form a bag it drew the flies with it and you could get the fish to follow and take when they hooked themselves in the scissors without fail. Half a dozen fish in an hour was usual with as many again lost through failing to hook or kicking off.

At the foot of this run was a shallow fall leading down to the middle estuary. Below the fall was a roundish pool with a gravel beach distinctly marked with a line of twigs showing to where the high tide reached. This was one of the best pools on the Teifi before the River Authority tore it apart with a mechanical grab. It was my favourite demonstration pool to which I often took summer visitors who had read a bit about sea-trout fishing and wanted to try. This was all free fishing apart from the statutory licence. It does seem rather quaint that the people who destroyed it were the ones getting the revenue from the licence. You had to be very inept indeed not to get a few plucks in this pool and even tyros often caught a fish.

From this point onwards the river became increasingly brackish when the tide was in. In the next mile there were only two places the angler could get down to fish due to the wooded nature of the gorge and the deep, very still, nature of the pools. The next fishing was not until the Teifi emerged on to the estuarial flats, took a plunge over a fell and some rock upcrops and rolled down a wide, deep glide a couple of hundred yards long which took the stream to the level of the salt marsh.

This glide always held fish and there were anglers who had taken up to a dozen sea-trout at each session from this one spot until their score was up over the hundred mark. The wading, however, was very dodgy and the whole place most difficult to reach except after half an hour's very hard walk. Most fortunately this productive glide was in view of an upper window of the bailiff's house on a nearby hill. Otherwise, nightly raids with illegal nets—which have been the curse of the Teifi for generations—would have culled the fish-crop before it even saw fresh water. However, there is nothing like a couple of Alsatians on the loose and a few thick-armed bailiffs around, well-versed in rough-house, to reduce the attractions of poaching. In those parts there were at least a couple of assaults on bailiffs every season— assaults mostly by men who supplemented their dole with a thriving netting racket.

Another estuary was quite different in character. The incoming saltwater was frustrated halfway up by the erection of a weir by the River Authority which had been fitted with a fish-pass that didn't work. The only time this fish-pass operated was on spring tides when there was plenty of water in the river. Lazy fishermen used to wander below this weir and fill a bag with sea-trout using a spinner. The Authority finally put up a notice forbidding fishing for 200 yards below the weir. It was repeatedly pointed out to them that this weir constituted an obstacle within the meaning of Common Law. Eventually they suggested building a Denzil channel to allow the fish to get upstream more easily. However when this idea was fed into the red tape network the Planning Authority objected. At the time of writing the fish are still obstructed on this estuary while clerks sharpen their quill pens and the ancient machinery of local government creaks on its appointed way. The fishing, meantime, has deteriorated to the extent that an annual catch of salmon 10 years ago for this little river of 40–50 fish has been converted into a 'catch' of 3 fish last year with sea-trout in like proportion. Some estuaries, it is only fair to say, have been ruined by those appointed to look after them.

The estuary fisher needs to take care that the swirls and boils under the far bank are indeed produced by sea-trout and not by mullet. Many hours are wasted each season by visitors casting to mullet that are not in taking mood under the mistaken impression that they were sea-trout. Yet it is not hard to observe the difference between the two rise-forms. Mullet are bolder and clumsier on the surface than sea-trout and tend to plough around making a visible wake perhaps for yards. Sea-trout, when they show on the top, are neater and quicker by half.

Lures

Remembering that brackish water sea-trout feed on small marine life-forms it would be a foolish mistake not to offer them the obvious lure, a slip of mackerel skin. Such slips are prepared in advance by taking a slice off a mackerel flank, turning it skin-side down and paring away all the flesh. Using a sharp pair of scissors cut leaf-shaped pieces from the skin about an inch long and fold them longitudinally while still moist. After this pack them in a tin box and cover with a felt pad moistened with a few drops of pilchard oil.

These lures are fished on fly-tackle by putting a lure on a plain hook and tying it in position with a bit of thread. A better method however is to obtain a few double or tandem hooks of the type used for dressing Worm flies and fit the slip on one of these. Mackerel slips are effective in freshwater as well as in estuaries and I suspect that quite a lot of 'fly-caught' sea-trout were, in fact, brought to their doom not by silk and feather but by mackerel skin. Gurnard skin is also very useful for this job.

These slips are particularly useful after dark because sea-trout have a habit of following a lure as it swings round in the current and investigating it closely. Part of this exercise, I feel sure, is to smell it. Obviously, artificial flies supply no stimulus at all to a fish doing this hence the need to provide something organic. It is this need that encourages people to use fly and maggot. But whether these tricks can be called 'fly-fishing' in the purist sense is open to doubt.

I was once invited to examine a huge sea-trout that had been caught with fly on fly-only water. The splendid fish was in deep-freeze at a local hotel. It only remained to congratulate the angling party involved. Shortly afterwards the catch earned an angling award for fly-fishing from a national newspaper. Only later did I learn that these anglers had arrived with spinning rods ready set up and this was probably the way the fish had been captured. If so, it not only broke the rules for the water but was dishonest to the newspaper concerned. All I can say is if you need material inducements in order to go fishing it is better to join a trawler crew.

Spinning of course is perfectly legitimate on most estuaries and it can be as interesting and nearly as effective as fly-fishing. There are vogues in spinning baits as in the case of women's hats. One firm used to produce an illogicality—a celluloid 'jacket' to cover the body of a spun natural minnow to save it from the teeth of the fish. It was warmly praised by some anglers of the period although the absurdity of using a real fish for bait and then covering it up to resemble an artificial seems to have struck no one. It is not a hard job to exchange a chewed-up natural minnow for a new one.

Devon minnows have headed the list of successful artificial baits for nearly a hundred years. They are successful because they are neat, simple in design and very effective. Devons have accounted for thousands of sea-trout and one can observe no end to the devon minnow saga. Quill minnows have also been highly successful and a lot of anglers will use nothing else. I must have caught many scores if not hundreds of sea-trout on quill minnows. The small size (about $1\frac{1}{2}$ inches long) is about the best and of the colour combinations I prefer brown and gold. A dealer who used to sell hundreds of quill minnows each season was very particular about the way he allowed them to leave his shop. He suspended each quill on a wire by the swivel at the nose and blew on the vanes. It had to spin easily and without wobble before he would okay it. Often the mount had to be adjusted or the flying treble made more secure. Personally I don't like flying trebles which seem to invite foul hooking and if I home-make a few quills I put only two trebles on them.

When is the best time to fish an estuary for sea-trout? I would say, without much doubt, during the week leading up to a full moon. This, of course, always coincides with a spring tide. Many—such as Ritz—have discussed the possibility that a solunar effect operates on fish in rivers. I am quite sure that there is such an effect, both in the estuary and in freshwater. Fish seem to be much more 'on the move' and actively feeding when the moon is waxing. Many experienced sea-trout fishers have commented on this and have proved the point by producing tables showing relative catches obtained during the waxing and waning phase of the moon. The effect could be gravitational but, whatever it is, it seems to affect the small organisms on which fish feed. Since gravity still remains largely a mystery there is really no way of being sure what actually takes place. Certainly it seems to influence moths and sedges and enormous hatches occur on warm evenings during the waxing stage. It probably also excites small sea organisms. There is no doubt that sea-trout run in far greater numbers during the waxing period but this may only be for the obvious reason that the tides are building up to greater size.

Fishing in the sea at an estuary mouth is well worth investigating especially during summer droughts when the abstractors have sucked their maximum quota from the river and it is possible to wade across the stream without wetting your ankles. Summer visitors to a small resort on a little sea-trout and salmon river some years ago were intrigued because the fish splashing around some seaweed-covered rocks appeared to be sea-trout. Word soon spread around and spinning accounted for quite a number before the fish found a safer place to play.

Which offers the best chance of making a basket of sea-trout—spinning or fly-fishing? This is a topic often fed into the conversation to liven it up and there is no doubt it usually does just that. Having done a fair amount of both I feel pretty sure that competent performers with the fly get the best deal. But why should this be so when both are fishing with lures, albeit of different sorts? I think that human as well as fish psychology comes into things in this matter even though there is a mechanical factor at work, too.

An artificial spinning bait is a one-time affair. The sea-trout either hits it and is hooked or it isn't. If not, then it never comes at it again. For this reason I like to use natural baits for spinning such as a small eel-tail or a natural minnow —whether fresh or preserved. Fresh shrimps are also good. An artificial fly is not always a one-time affair. Sea-trout will often come a second time at a fly provided they have not been pricked. On the first attack they may have merely tweaked the wing of the fly or perhaps tried to drown it by flipping water over it with their tail the way they often do with sedges and other big insects.

The psychological aspect is interesting. Many dedicated spinners for sea-trout have no time to waste. Their line criss-crosses the water and they move on quickly to the next pool to repeat the process. I have seen people fish three or four miles of river in an afternoon giving some pools no more than a few cursory throws. I have also seen people spin a stretch very methodically and do no good. The reason is that at some stage they have pricked a fish without knowing it and have alarmed every taking sea-trout in the area. Drawing a blank they move elsewhere and perhaps do the same again only to end up complaining that there are no fish up.

Some years ago I tried an experiment on a well-fished run which I knew always held fish. It was about 100 yards long with one side tree-shaded and both sides hemmed in by 6-foot high banks. The nearside was wadeable with care. The fish lay on the other, deeper, side. Beginning at the top I fished down slowly, taking half an hour about it, and had one fish of about 1¼ lb. Some spinning anglers arrived to watch so I then sat on the bank and let them go ahead. In ten minutes they had combed the water from every angle and had drawn a blank. Soon afterwards they moved away to spin further water.

I gave the run a good rest and then waded in for a second time. On this occasion I had two fish, a smaller one than the first and one slightly larger. From the level of the water and general condition of the river it was obvious that there were substantial numbers of sea-trout under the trees opposite and it was simply a case of showing patience. Sure enough, more spinning fishers arrived and I moved back to let them have a crack. They hooked exactly nothing and expressed the opinion that I must have caught the lot.

This same situation occurred at least three times and always with the same result. In the end, feeling tired and having all the fish I needed, I packed up. This was after a spectator joined me—a visitor with a fly-rod—who watched me grapple with two at once, a nice sea-trout on the top dropper and a smaller one on the point-fly. After this I left him to it even though the fish were still taking and a further run down the pool would certainly have resulted in more takes.

When fishing the fly in these conditions it is important to fish slowly and methodically. A splashy delivery or a lot of false casting only alarms the sea-trout. I like to make a single false cast before dropping the fly exactly where it is to go—in this case it was about 6 inches from the opposite bank. All this, of course, was daylight and early evening fishing. After dark it is not possible to estimate the length of the cast so exactly, nor is it necessary. Darkness lends sea-trout a measure of boldness.

One of the most curious incidents I ever experienced in an estuary was one night in an overgrown part of the Teifi gorge. I was using a cast of small double-hook flies and had already taken one fish. Suddenly, I hooked a whopper. The situation was difficult because the light had almost gone and I had no torch. Moreover the tide had started to ebb and the stream was coming down at a great rate. Much too early and too hard I put some pressure on the fish and this is often fatal with small doubles as it was on this occasion—the hooks pulled out. At that precise moment two coracles swept down out of the dark, net suspended between them, and automatically picked up the fish I had just lost. Coracle-netting is still permitted on a few rivers and this was one of them. I had a split second, as they raced past, to see that the fish was a fine one of 5–6 lb. An instant later they were past, taking my lost fish with them into the darkness.

Sea-trout fishing in estuaries is not all bending rods and loaded baskets. It can be tiresome and difficult. Marine weed can render fishing quite abortive. But nothing lasts for ever and it is the good times we remember when memory recalls estuary days.

Index

Allis shad, 121
Anchors, 27
Anoraks, 13
Artificial baits, 63

Bait 'cocktails', 61
Bait collecting, 55
Baited spoon for flounders, 94
Baits
　for bass, 78
　for cod, 106
　for brill, 102
　for codling, 108
　for drift lining, 33
　for mullet, 84, 87
　for plaice, 96
　for whiting, 110
　natural v. artificial, 17, 30
Bass, 68 et seq.
　netting, 76
　tagging, 76
Bells, on rods, 78
Birds
　estuarine, 8
　as fish indicators, 73
Black lug, 56
Blood knots, 53
Blue shark, 9
Boat, choice of, 25
Boat fishing, 25 et seq.
　for bass, 71
　for plaice, 98
　for turbot, 101
　for whiting, 112
Boats
　launching, 27
　towing behind car, 26
Bonito, 123
Bores, tidal, 9

Brass wire, 43
'Breakaway' leads, 52
Brill, 102 et seq.
Brit, shoals of, 72
Bubble-float, 87

Camping, 13
'Capta' leads, 52
Centre-pin reels, 29
Channels in estuaries, 18
Choosing a boat, 25
Chromed brass wire, 51
Clement's boom, 43
Clothing, 13
Coalfish, 115
Coarse fish, 10
Cockles, as bait, 61
Cod, 105 et seq.
Codling, 108 et seq.
Collars, on lines, 15
Commercial fishing for bass, 81
Commercialism, 37
Conservation, 38
Cooking mullet, 90
Crab-board, 59
Crab-infested ground, 48
Crabs, as bait, 59
Crawling leger, 94

Dab, lemon, 103
Dabs, 99 et seq.
　in shallow water, 19
Definition of estuary, 7
Dinghies, 25
　launching, 27
Drift lining, 20, 33

Eel drag, 102
Eel rake, 102

139

Engines, outboard, 27
Estuaries
  as nurseries, 10
  coarse fishing in, 10
  General description, 7
  marks in, 29

Feathered lures, 32, 63
Fish, as bait for bass, 75
  order of entering estuaries, 19
Fishing
  a brit shoal, 74
  for cod, 106
  for codling, 108
  for mackerel, 117, 120
  for mullet, 88
  for turbot, 101
  for whiting, 111
  rights, 11
Flatfish, special rigs for, 49
Flies
  for mackerel, 118
  for mullet, 89
  for sea-trout, 129
Float fishing, 48
  for mullet, 87
Flounders, 92 *et seq.*
  in shallow water, 19
Flounder traps, wire netting, 93
Flowing traces, 50
Fly-fishing
  for mackerel, 118
  for mullet, 86, 89
  for sea-trout, 128
  for slob trout, 126
Food
  of brill, 102
  of cod, 105
  of dabs, 99
  of flounders, 93
  of mullet, 84
  of plaice, 96
  of soles, 103
  of sea-trout, 127
  of turbot, 100
  of whiting, 110

Fuel for engines, 28

Gammon, Clive, 86
Garfish, 125
Garrad, John P., 87, 94
'German Sprat', 34, 67
Greater sand-eel, 58
Grip leads, 46
Ground fishing, 32
Gurnard-skin lures, 134

Haddock, 109
Halibut, 100, 104
Hermit crabs, 62
Herrings, 118 *et seq.*
Hooks, 30, 47

Jardine leads, 52

Kennedy, Michael, 84, 89, 96
Killer whales, 9
Killicks, 36
King rag, 57
Knots, 53

Landlocked mullet, 86
Lasks, 33
Launce, 58
  artificial, 65
  in estuaries, 71
Leads, 46 *et seq.*
  for bass surf fishing, 78
  making, 51
Leger tackle, 42
Lemon dab, 103
Lemon sole, 103 *et seq.*
Licences, 11
Lines
  shore fishing, 15
  spinning, 16
Live bait, 33
Long liner's hook, 48
Long-shanked hooks, 31
Lowestoft Fisheries Laboratory, 76
Lugworms, 55

Lures
  for bass, 79
  for herrings, 120
  for sea-trout, 132

Mackerel, 116 *et seq.*
Mackerel lasks, 33
Maps, use of, 8
Megrims, 104
Monofil, suggested strengths, 53
Moulds for leads, 46
Movements
  of cod, 105
  of whiting, 110
Mullet, 82 *et seq.*
  in fresh water, 90
  species of, 82
Mussels, as bait, 60

Natural baits, 76
Netting
  bass, 76
  mullet, 90

Outboard engines, 27

Paddleworm, 64
Paste bait for mullet, 87
Paternosters, 44
Paternoster
  and ledger combination, 32
  booms, 43
Peeler crabs, 59
Pelamid, 123
Pike, 10
Pirks, 32, 65
Plaice, 96 *et seq.*
Plastic sand-eels, 36
Plugs, 66
Pollack, 115
Porpoises, 19
Pouting, 114
Prawns, 62

Quill minnows, 134

Ragworms, 57
Razorfish, 61
'Red Gill' sand-eel, 36, 64
Red lug, 56
Red mullet, 82
Reels
  cleaning, 16
  shore fishing, 14
Ribbon worms, 57
Rod rings, 14
Rods, shore fishing, 14
Rolling leger, 50
  for flounders, 93
Rubber eels, 64

Sand-eels, 33
  as bait, 58
  artificial, 34, 36
    to make, 65
  baiting with, 71
Screw links, 43
Sea Angler's Fishes, The, 84
Sea Angling with a Baited Spoon, 94
Sea slaters, 58
Sea mouse, 57
Sea-trout, 127 *et seq.*
  fly *v.* spinner experiment, 135
  locations of, 130
Seals, 9, 10
Seine-nets, 37
Shad, 121
Shellfish, as bait, 60
Shore fishing
  choice of position, 18
  for plaice, 98
  for turbot, 101
Shrimps, 62
Slipper limpets, 55
Slob trout, 126 *et seq.*
Softback crabs, 59
Soles, 102
Solunar theory, 134
Spiney cockles, 61
Spinning baits, natural *v.* artificial, 17

141

Spinning
  for bass, 79
  for sea-trout, 133
  from a boat, 35
  lures, 36
  tackle, 16
Spoons, to make, 67
Spiral leads, 52
Spreader arms, 43
Stainless steel
  hooks, 47
  wire, 43
Sturgeon in River Towy, 122
Sub-tropical visitors, 123
'Super-bass', 75
Surf casting end tackle, 41
Surf fishing for bass, 77
Swedish spoons, 67
Swivels, grease for, 17

Tackle
  for brill, 102
  for cod, 106
  for codling, 108
  for flounders, 94
  for ground fishing, 31
  for herrings, 119
  for mackerel, 117
  for mullet, 85
  for plaice, 97
  for soles, 103
  for turbot, 101
  for whiting, 111
  spinning, 16
Terminal rigs, 40
Terylene lines, 35
Tides
  effect on feeding bass, 69
  warning about, 8
Trace, spinning, 16
Trailers, 27
Trawling, 37, 38
  for plaice, 97
Trigger fish, 9, 124
Trolling, 34
Trolling a sand-eel, 71
Turbot, 100 *et seq.*
Twaite shad, 121

Vibration in lures, 37

Waders, 13
Wading, warning about, 77
Warm water outfalls, 80
Whiting, 110 *et seq.*
Wire-netting flounder traps, 93
Witches, 99
Worms, to hook, 56
Wreck fishing, 29

Zones, sea, 34